Table of Contents

AF149859

Plosive Consonants (6)

Nasal Consonants (3) and Nasal Plosions (2)

Lateral consonants (1) and Lateral Plosions (2)

Fricative Consonants (10)

Affricates (2)

Get Rid of your Accent

THE ENGLISH PRONUNCIATION AND ARTICULATION TRAINING MANUAL

By Linda James and Olga Smith

"As a diplomat I need effective communication skills, particularly to address public audiences through radio and TV. A clear, crisp accent is always more convincing than a thick, foreign one. I am reading this book and I think it is immensely useful for foreigners like myself."
Samuel Moncada, Venezuelan Ambassador to the UK

"Precise, concise, compelling, comprehensive, achieving its targets, witty, well written and beautifully spoken, this book is a must for every student, every actor and every individual aiming for a better living and a better life in Britain and elsewhere."
John Kennedy Melling, Fellow of the Institute of Chartered Accountants, Fellow of the Royal Society of Art, author, broadcaster and critic.

"This is a fabulous book! I'm a management accountant, but because of my strong Polish accent, I sometimes felt that people were treating me like the kebab woman. Now, I listen to the CDs and practice and can see my progress; the method and exercises in the book are really working for me."
Anna Tunc, UK immigrant from Poland

"Clearly, the authors of the book have collected years of experience and expertise to create this practical and effective tool for speech study."
Joe Windley, Head of Speech, Central School of Speech and Drama, London

"The book has proven invaluable in one to one teaching, allowing me to focus on the student's problem areas. I have also used it with success in a group environment. There is sufficient material to provide meaningful practice of each sound, with enough variety to keep students entertained."
Marianne Gibson, teacher, St. George International College, London

"This is by far the best pronunciation book I have ever had -- and, believe you me, I have bought and used numerous of them. The main author is evidently an expert in teaching pronunciation. The recorded exercises are excellent, too. I highly recommend this book! I am very glad that I came across it!"
JV Barrios Nunez, Berkshire, England, Amazon.co.uk reader

Published by Olga Smith, Business & Technical Communication Services, 8 Fairholme Road, London, W14 9JX

Information on this title and on accent reduction courses: www.batcs.co.uk

Seventh Edition

Toppan Printing Co. (Shenzhen) Ltd, No.27 Industrial Zone Chuangye Road, Boan, Shenzhen, 518133 China

Introduction

What is an accent?

An accent identifies which part of the country or part of the world you come from. There are different types of accents: Scottish, Russian, Spanish; educated, strong, slight; and many others.

According to the Rough Guide to England, "England is a country where accent and vocabulary can stamp a person's identity like a brand." Indeed, the biggest single factor that affects people's first impression of you is your speech and accent.

Why do we speak with different accents?

From childhood we learn to speak by imitating our relatives, teachers and friends. The way we speak and our pronunciation are influenced by the environment we live in.

Sounds are created by our speech organs, namely the lips, tongue and jaw. The positions of our speech organs are different for different sounds. For example, we drop the tongue in order to pronounce the English [æ] sound as in "cat". In order to pronounce [w] as in "way" we put our lips in a tight whistle, and then pull them back sharply.

Many people begin to learn English when they are adults. They may not automatically position their speech organs as native English speakers will. Moreover, they often don't know how to correctly position their speech organs in order to produce clear English sounds, because not all English sounds exist in other languages.

For example, there is no [w] in Russian, and many Russians pronounce [v] instead of [w]. Another example is that Russian lacks long vowels, and therefore there is a natural tendency for Russians to shorten long English vowels and diphthongs. Instead of "two sheets of paper" they most likely will pronounce "two shits of paper". Instead of saying "the room is dark", they are likely to pronounce "the room is duck".

Speaking, writing and listening are taught in most colleges, but phonetics and pronunciation classes are not always part of the curriculum. Even when they are, they tend to be very basic, focusing more on conversation than phonetics.

Is it important to have good pronunciation?

Just consider the following points.

Bad pronunciation:
- May be confusing and hard to understand for those who listen to you
- Gives the impression that you are uneducated
- Can be an obstacle in your work or studies
- Doesn't allow you to become a good public speaker.

Good pronunciation and a neutral accent:
- Allows you to become a pleasant communicator
- Is a good basis for public speaking
- Will enable you to enjoy speaking more
- Gives you confidence, and your confidence in turn opens up for you all sorts of opportunities.

Is it possible to reduce or eliminate an accent?

The earlier we start to pronounce English properly, the less accent we have. It's more difficult to reduce or completely eliminate an accent when you are older. However, it is not impossible. It all depends on your hard work, perseverance, high quality professional training and – last, but not least – on using the appropriate book with a sound track.

Why Received Pronunciation?

Why not learn to speak with a Scottish or London Cockney accent? Why make an effort to reduce a strong Russian or Spanish accent? The reason is very simple: to help you with making your English clear and easy to understand for the majority of English-speaking people.

This book teaches you how to develop Received Pronunciation (RP). RP is simply a neutral pronunciation of educated Southern English. It's sometimes called Standard English.

Beginning over a century ago, RP spread rapidly throughout the Civil Service of the British Empire and became the voice of authority and power in a substantial part of the world. Because it was a regionally 'neutral' accent, and was thought to be more widely understood than any regional accent, it also came to be adopted by the BBC when radio broadcasting began in the 1920s.

The first Director General of the BBC, Lord Reith, when asked why he had chosen RP for the BBC, replied: "I tried to get a style or quality of English which would not be laughed at in any part of the country."

To date RP retains its considerable status. It is still the standard accent of Parliament, the Church of England, the High Courts and other British national institutions. It has long been the chief accent taught to foreigners who wish to learn a British model. RP is also taught in acting schools in the UK, as actors from different cultural and social backgrounds are required to have the ability to speak using RP when it's necessary for their performances.

It should be noted that RP is not static. Modern RP has been simplified compared to, say, what it was over 50 years ago, and now sounds more neutral and democratic. However, it will most certainly remain the accent of educated people.

Why we wrote this book

To date you can only get speech training in British drama schools or if you take speech lessons from a private speech tutor. We wanted to make this exclusive training accessible for a much wider audience. We took the method long used in London drama schools, adapted it for learners of English and collated it into a single training manual, the first of its kind.

You will find that you will get from the book what you put into your work with it. The exercises are quite intensive and will require you to work hard at your pronunciation. But, the book isn't just a study tool; we have also tried to make it amusing and interesting. Have fun, and remember that your hard work will be rewarded in full!

Three things that make our book special

- Tried and trusted method in eliminating an accent
- Fun yet very effective speech training
- Amusing vocabulary

Methodology used in this book

In our book, we set out a complete method of learning English sounds, which someone who comes from a different country might not have in their own native language.

One of the important things about our book is that we make it absolutely clear what is happening in the mouth: where the lips go, where the tongue is placed, if the jaw is open or closed, etc. Once those three positions are checked and sorted out then there is no way that you could not make that particular English sound.

The second important part of speech training is training the muscles of the tongue, lips and jaw, so that the brain responds automatically. You train them by pronouncing words and sentences with the target sound. You finish with a little bit of verse, something interesting and amusing, but also containing the target sound.

For consonants we also give practice through articulation exercises, such as period verses and tongue-twisters, which get the tongue and the lips really moving so that we get clarity and crispness of speech. English is a very energetic and dynamic language, and good articulation makes a big difference.

Exercises in the book are accompanied by a sound track on the CD. Students should listen to the CD, practice the correct sound throughout, and then record themselves and listen to the recording in order to see their progress. We also encourage students to use the correct sounds in their everyday speech, and support learning with additional exercises at the end of each lesson.

The CD was recorded by professional actors who use drama techniques in order to make the sentences, verses and poems sound interesting and amusing. This also helps you to use your imagination as you are reading, and that will help you to memorise sounds.

The lessons in this book are quite intensive and are aimed for those who strive to achieve outstanding results in improving their accents within a short period of time. Your results might depend on your ability to hear your own speech and the time you spend mastering the sounds.

At the end of the book we also provide students with instructions and advice on how to maintain correct pronunciation. In support of that we give a warm-up exercise for all the English sounds (see page 121).

Students will also find a table of particular difficulties with the English pronunciation which speakers of other world languages have (see page 125).

English spelling and pronunciation

In many languages letters of the alphabet are pronounced in the same way as they are spelled. However, the English language was, at different times, under French, German and Dutch influence. English inherited and includes many foreign words. This is one of the reasons why there are so many exceptions to the rule in pronunciation and spelling.

The characteristic peculiarity of the English language is that the same letter of the alphabet can be pronounced differently. For example, the letter "a" in the word "father" is pronounced as a long vowel [ɑ:], but in the word "man" it is a short vowel sound [æ]. In the word "among", where it's not stressed, it is a neutral vowel or schwa [ə]. Thus the letter "a" can be pronounced in at least three different ways.

Another difficulty is that the same English sounds have different spellings. For example, diphthong [ɪə] has several spellings: in the word 'fear' it is spelled as 'ear', in the word 'weird' it is spelled as 'eir'.

Although we highlight the practiced sound in bold and offer different spelling variations for the same sound, we should point out that there can be other spelling variations for the same sound. Therefore, when you learn a new word you should always consult a dictionary for the correct phonetic pronunciation.

Who this book is for

The book enables people to develop clear and precise English speech, and to neutralise their foreign or their British regional accent. Both native and non-native English speakers will benefit from the book.

Native English speakers include:
- Pronunciation and speech teachers
- Actors with non-RP accents who wish to pursue an acting career in the UK
- Hollywood actors who need to develop a British accent
- Professionals for whom a high standard of English and clarity of speech are important.

Non-native English speakers include:
- Students
- International businessmen and executives
- Diplomats
- Call centre employees
- Intelligence agents
- Skilled professionals: teachers, professors, doctors, journalists etc who wish to advance in their profession in Britain, the United States, Canada, Australia and other countries where English is an official or business language (e.g. India)
- People who work in service and hospitality industries and need to communicate using good English.

Method of learning

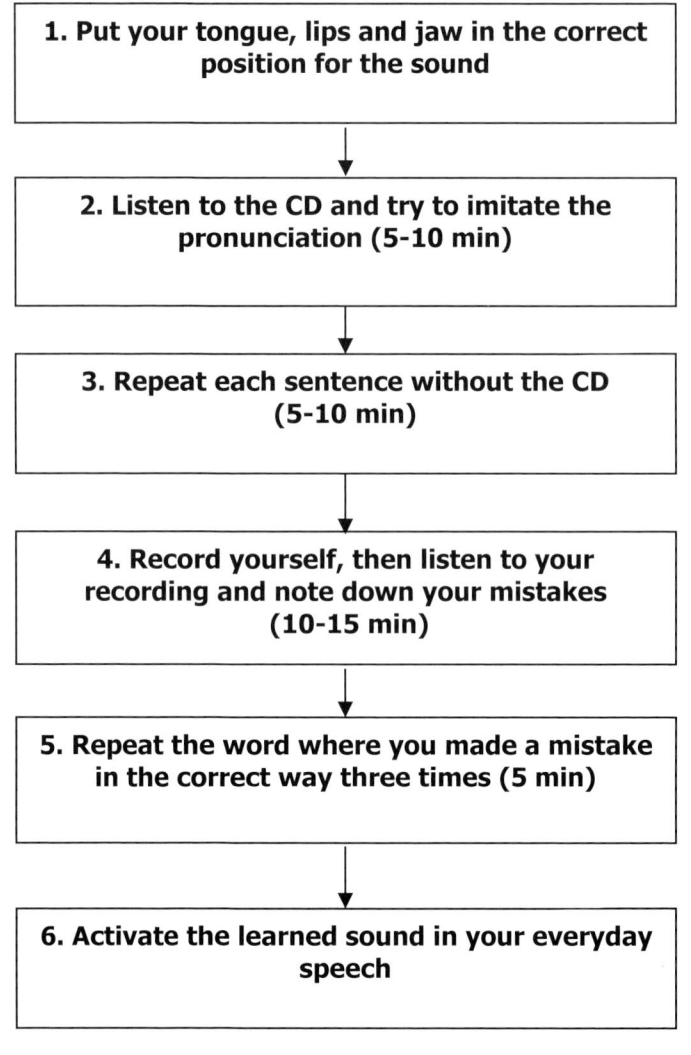

1. Put your tongue, lips and jaw in the correct position for the sound

2. Listen to the CD and try to imitate the pronunciation (5-10 min)

3. Repeat each sentence without the CD (5-10 min)

4. Record yourself, then listen to your recording and note down your mistakes (10-15 min)

5. Repeat the word where you made a mistake in the correct way three times (5 min)

6. Activate the learned sound in your everyday speech

Explanation of the method of learning

What is needed to start working with the book?
- A mirror, to compare the shape of your own mouth to the shape of the mouth that you will find in diagrams at the beginning of each lesson;
- A recorder, to record your practices;
- A CD player.

See page 117 for a labelled diagram of speech organs.

How many hours you should spend on each sound:
- Practice each sound for about 20-40 minutes a day, with little breaks in between;
- Repeat on the following days for approximately the same length of time until you feel that you can use the correct sound in your everyday speech.

As shown on the previous page the method of learning is based on a six-stage process:

The first stage is to make sure that you put your lips, tongue and jaw in the right position for the learned sound. If you fail to do so, the sound will not be precise and may be different altogether. Follow the instructions on speech organ position given at the beginning of each lesson. Pronounce the sound several times, looking in the mirror to make sure you do it correctly. When you feel that your sound is correct, start pronouncing the words, sentences and verses in the lesson.

The second stage is aimed at helping you learn a sound by repeating and imitating after the tape. This exercise will help you to make the sound as correctly as possible and train your speech organs for the particular sound. The more you repeat after the tape, the better your pronunciation becomes.

The third stage gives you an opportunity to practice the sound on your own, without the help of the tape. You will be hearing yourself and mastering the sound. This stage is essential before recording yourself.

The fourth stage involves recording yourself and listening to the recording. It helps you to see whether you have progressed in mastering the pronunciation and to identify where you still make mistakes.

The fifth stage focuses on eliminating mistakes. Correctly repeating the words where you made a mistake will help you avoid repeating the same mistakes in the future.

The sixth stage has the purpose of helping you incorporate the learned sound in everyday speech. It's about trying to find the learned sound in the newspapers, on the radio, on TV and in English language videos. Pay attention to how you pronounce the learned sound in your everyday speech. This will help you to activate the correctly pronounced sounds.

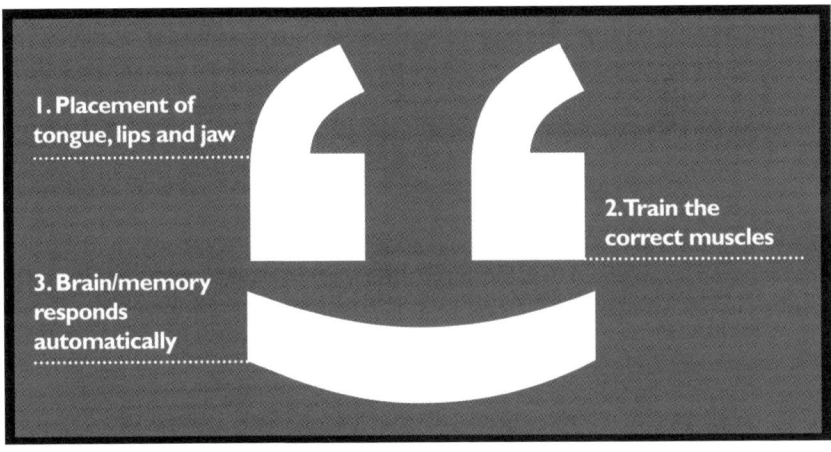

Intonation

Intonation/inflexion is a gentle rise and fall of the voice within a sentence. Experienced speech tutors have come to the conclusion that it's very challenging to teach, because each person will involuntarily assume the tune of their native language. It is very deeply ingrained in a person. Emotion and meaning will inevitably change the levels of pitch in the voice. Learners of Received Pronunciation are advised to listen to native English speakers on audio books, CDs, at the movies, in the theatre etc., and try to copy not only the pronunciation, but also the tune of the voice, or intonation.

Stress

The English language is composed of words with varied stresses. All words when said in isolation, and most words when in a connected passage, have at least one stressed syllable. When we combine words into sentences, the words retain their individual stresses, but because of the meaning the speaker wants to convey, certain complete words are stressed as well. For example:

1. Linda walked to the theatre with **Michael**. By putting a stress on "Michael", we emphasise that Linda walked to the theatre with Michael, and not with John or somebody else.

2. Linda **walked** to the theatre with Michael. By putting a stress on "walked" we emphasise that Linda walked to the theatre, and did not, for example, ride or cycle.

3. Linda walked to the **theatre** with Michael. By putting a stress on "theatre", we emphasise that Linda walked to the theatre, and not to the cinema or a concert.

4. **Linda** walked to the theatre with Michael. By putting a stress on "Linda", we emphasise that it was Linda who walked to the theatre with Michael, and not somebody else.

The above examples demonstrate that sentence stress depends on the meaning we wish to convey and that there is no particular rule to follow. Stress comes from a combination of several factors – extra loudness of sounds, extra length of sounds and a change of pitch in the voice.

Recommendations

The sentences in "Get Rid of your Accent" are recorded by professional actors, who have made an effort to make the sentences interesting and expressive, with a bit of a drama effect. It would be immensely helpful to imitate their intonation/inflection and stress if you would like to sound more English.

Lesson 1: The [ɑ:] sound as in "bark"

Speech organs position:

Open jaw, relaxed lips;
flat tongue pulled back a little.
The sound is made in the back
of the mouth.

[ɑ: ɑ: ɑ:]

A1
🎧 Words

Listen and repeat. Look at the mouth diagram to help you position your lips, tongue and jaw for the target sound.

Spelling variations for the [ɑ:] sound	Highlighted bold letters pronounced as [ɑ:]
ar ("r" is silent)	**ar**t, **ar**ms, b**ar**, m**ar**k, **ar**ch, b**ar**k, d**ar**k
ear, er, al, au	h**ear**t, s**er**geant, cl**er**k, D**er**by, ps**al**m, l**au**gh
a before **s, n** and **th**	b**a**th, c**a**stle, f**a**st, gl**a**ss, dis**a**ster, r**a**ther, enh**a**nce

A2
🎧 Sentences

Listen and repeat. Read each sentence aloud slowly at first, then as if you were telling it to someone in a natural way.

1. The **mar**ble bird-b**a**th was hidden in the tall gr**a**sses near the p**a**th.
2. Let's p**ar**k our **car** at **Bar**bara's as the **car** p**ar**k is r**a**ther f**ar** from the theatre.
3. At l**a**st M**ar**garet's anxiety p**a**ssed and she ch**a**nced a dis**a**strous d**a**nce with a l**au**ghing s**er**geant.
4. I'd r**a**ther take a ch**a**nce and let my f**a**ther drive me to the garage in his f**a**st **car**.
5. H**ar**d-h**ear**ted M**ar**garet was reading ps**al**ms in the d**ar**k.
6. As an office boy I made such a m**ar**k that I was given the post of a junior cl**er**k.

12

A3
🎧 Verses

Listen and copy the intonation and voice modulation on the CD.

Barbara's **car** is a Jaguar
And B**ar**bara drives r**a**ther f**a**st.
C**a**stles, f**ar**ms and dr**au**ghty b**ar**ns,
She goes ch**ar**ging p**a**st.

When I, good friends, was called to the b**ar**,
I'd an appetite fresh and h**ear**ty,
But I was, as many barristers **are**,
An impecunious p**ar**ty.
(W.S. Gilbert)

Additional exercises:

A: *Write down 4 words with the target sound that you often use when speaking English. Practice these words, thinking about your lips, tongue and jaw positions for the target sound.*

1. _____ 3. _____

2. _____ 4. _____

B: *Write down 4 words with the target sound that you often hear on TV, radio or from your friends/colleagues. Practice these words, thinking about your lips, tongue and jaw positions for the target sound.*

1. _____ 3. _____

2. _____ 4. _____

Lesson 2: The [u:] sound as in "boot"

Speech organs position:
Jaw is almost closed,
lips pushed forward tightly
into a whistle shape;
the back of the tongue
rises up towards the soft
palate at the back of the mouth.

[u: u: u:]

A4
🎧 Words

Listen and repeat. Look at the mouth diagram to help you position your lips, tongue and jaw for the target sound.

Spelling variations for the [u:] sound	Highlighted bold letters pronounced as [u:]
oo	bloom, food, smooth, loop, school, doom
o	lose, move, do, who, improvement, remove
ue, oe	blue, glue, shoes
ui	fruit, juice, cruise
Spelling variations for the [ju:] sound	Highlighted bold letters pronounced as [ju:]
u	tune, tube, music, curious, tulips
ew	new, few, Kew, mews

A5
🎧 Sentences

Listen and repeat. Read each sentence aloud slowly at first, then as if you were telling it to someone in a natural way.

1. Ruth felt in tune with the cool of a June evening and admired the beauty of the moon.
2. There are quite a few music super-stars on the London tube.
3. These new blue shoes look beautiful with a navy blue coat.
4. On our cruise to Bermuda we played snooker with our schooner crew.
5. Coolies are made from juicy fruits and sugar.
6. The music tutor sang a tune on Tuesday for the duke.

14

7. A f**ew** b**eau**tiful t**u**lips gr**ew** in the sch**oo**l garden in J**u**ly.

Listen and copy the intonation and voice modulation on the CD.

I'd a swallow-tail coat of a b**eau**tiful bl**ue** -
A brief which I bought off a b**oo**by
A couple of shirts and a collar or t**wo**,
And a ring that looked like a r**u**by!

We sail the ocean bl**ue**,
And our saucy ship's a b**eau**ty;
We're sober men and tr**ue**,
And attentive to our b**eau**ty.
(*W.S. Gilbert*)

Additional exercises:

A: *Write down 4 words with the target sound that you often use when speaking English. Practice these words, thinking about your lips, tongue and jaw positions for the target sound.*

1. _____ 3. _____

2. _____ 4. _____

B: *Write down 4 words with the target sound that you often hear on TV, radio or from your friends/colleagues. Practice these words, thinking about your lips, tongue and jaw positions for the target sound.*

1. _____ 3. _____

2. _____ 4. _____

Lesson 3: The [ɔ:] sound as in "fort"

Speech organs position:
Open jaw, lips are slightly rounded and pushed forward. The back of the tongue rises at the back of the mouth.

[ɔ: ɔ: ɔ:]

A7
🎧 Words

Listen and repeat. Look at the mouth diagram to help you position your lips, tongue and jaw for the target sound.

Spelling variations for the [ɔ:] sound	Highlighted bold letters pronounced as [ɔ:]
or	st**or**m, d**oor**, h**or**se, c**or**pulent, s**or**did, **or**ganic
aw	**aw**e, l**aw**, d**aw**n, l**aw**n, spr**aw**l
au	c**au**stic, P**au**l, c**au**tious
augh	n**augh**ty, h**augh**ty, d**augh**ter
a before **l** and **al**	**al**most, b**al**l, w**al**l, w**al**k, t**al**k, app**al**ling, **al**though

A8
🎧 Sentences

Listen and repeat. Read each sentence aloud slowly at first, then as if you were telling it to someone in a natural way.

1. Ge**or**ge was f**al**ling asleep **aw**kwardly in a spr**aw**l.
2. The written **law**s **ough**t to prevent th**ough**tless t**al**ks.
3. This app**al**ling st**or**e was full of **al**l s**or**ts of **or**dinary sh**or**ts.
4. M**au**d's d**augh**ter Ge**or**gina was an **aw**ful d**augh**ter-in-l**aw**.
5. F**our** hundred and f**or**ty-f**our** st**or**ks flying home in the st**or**m.
6. P**au**l c**al**led out when he th**ough**t he s**aw** his n**augh**ty d**augh**ter f**al**l in the w**a**ter.

16

A9
🎧 Verses

Listen and copy the intonation and voice modulation on the CD.

As I was going by Mr King's yard,
I s**aw** a man s**aw**ing,
And of **all** the s**aw**yers I ever s**aw**,
I never s**aw** a s**aw** s**aw** like that s**aw**
s**aw**ed.

Additional exercises:

A: *Write down 4 words with the target sound that you often use when speaking English. Practice these words, thinking about your lips, tongue and jaw positions for the target sound.*

1. _____ 3. _____

2. _____ 4. _____

B: *Write down 4 words with the target sound that you often hear on TV, radio or from your friends/colleagues. Practice these words, thinking about your lips, tongue and jaw positions for the target sound.*

1. _____ 3. _____

2. _____ 4. _____

Lesson 4: The [iː] sound as in "feet"

Speech organs position:

Jaw is almost closed,
lips are spread; the front of
the tongue is high and forward
in the mouth.

[iː   iː   iː]

A10
𝆕 Words

Listen and repeat. Look at the mouth diagram to help you position your lips, tongue and jaw for the target sound.

Spelling variations for the [iː] sound	Highlighted bold letters pronounced as [iː]
ee	keel, feeble, seek, heed, see, peep, feel
e	he, evening, eve, demonise, Peter, these
ea	meat, tea, leave, jeans, please, team
ie	grief, field, relief, believe
ei	receipt, deceit, seize

A11
𝆕 Sentences

Listen and repeat. Read each sentence aloud slowly at first, then as if you were telling it to someone in a natural way.

1. One evening, lying by the stream on the green grass, I dreamed of eating sweets.
2. Jean, have you been in a wheat field in Leek?
3. His demeanour seems to reveal the secret reasons for his deceit.
4. Demonised teenagers were pleased with their tea.
5. All legal furies seize you! No proposal seems to please you.
6. I believe my feet are really quite clean, Evie.

18

A12
🎧 Verses

Listen and copy the intonation and voice modulation on the CD.

S**ee** – s**ee** – they drink
All thought unh**ee**ding,
The t**ea**-cups clink,
They are exc**ee**ding!

Additional exercises:

A: *Write down 4 words with the target sound that you often use when speaking English. Practice these words, thinking about your lips, tongue and jaw positions for the target sound.*

1. _____ 3. _____

2. _____ 4. _____

B: *Write down 4 words with the target sound that you often hear on TV, radio or from your friends/colleagues. Practice these words, thinking about your lips, tongue and jaw positions for the target sound.*

1. _____ 3. _____

2. _____ 4. _____

Lesson 5: The [ɜː] sound as in "third"

Speech organs position:
Jaw is half-open, relaxed lips;
the middle of the tongue
rises slightly.

[ɜː   ɜː   ɜː]

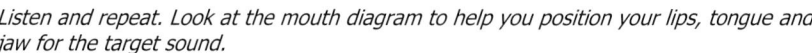

A13
🎧 Words

Listen and repeat. Look at the mouth diagram to help you position your lips, tongue and jaw for the target sound.

Spelling variations for the [ɜː] sound	Highlighted bold letters pronounced as [ɜː]
er	p**er**jury, comm**er**cial, w**er**e, v**er**se, inf**er**nal
ir	sh**ir**t, f**ir**st, st**ir**, g**ir**l, S**ir**, b**ir**d
ear	y**ear**n, **ear**n, p**ear**l
ur	**ur**ge, occ**ur**, m**ur**muring, b**ur**den, f**ur**nace, b**ur**n
or	w**or**k, w**or**se, w**or**ld, w**or**d

A14
🎧 Sentences

Listen and repeat. Read each sentence aloud slowly at first, then as if you were telling it to someone in a natural way.

1. The g**ir**ls in p**ur**ple sh**ir**ts w**er**e **ur**ged not to dist**ur**b S**ir** Cuthbert.
2. This p**ur**ple sh**ir**t is the w**or**st in the w**or**ld! I have no w**or**ds!
3. We w**er**e w**or**king in the W**or**ld Bank at f**ir**st; then we w**er**e transf**er**red to the Comm**er**cial Chambers in P**er**th.
4. My boyfriend is a p**er**fect n**er**d who makes his **ear**nings when everyone else is yearning.
5. The g**ir**l h**ear**d that she came th**ir**d in the W**or**ld Championships as a h**ur**dler.
6. **Ur**sula obs**er**ved that the boy w**or**e a d**ir**ty p**ur**ple j**er**sey.

A15
🎧 Verses

Listen and copy the intonation and voice modulation on the CD.

When I was a lad I s**er**ved a t**er**m
As office boy to an Att**or**ney's f**ir**m.

The rich att**or**ney was good as his w**or**d;
And every day my voice was h**ear**d
At the Sessions of Ancient Bailey.
(*W.S. Gilbert*)

Additional exercises:

A: *Write down 4 words with the target sound that you often use when speaking English. Practice these words, thinking about your lips, tongue and jaw positions for the target sound.*

1. _____ 3. _____

2. _____ 4. _____

B: *Write down 4 words with the target sound that you often hear on TV, radio or from your friends/colleagues. Practice these words, thinking about your lips, tongue and jaw positions for the target sound.*

1. _____ 3. _____

2. _____ 4. _____

Lesson 6: The [ə] neutral vowel (schwa) as in "the"

Speech organs position:

Jaw is half-open, relaxed
lips; the middle of the tongue
rises slightly. The sound
is very short.

[ə   ə   ə]

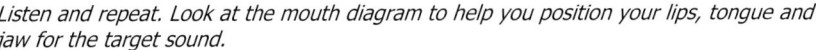

A16
🎧 Words

Listen and repeat. Look at the mouth diagram to help you position your lips, tongue and jaw for the target sound.

	Highlighted bold letters pronounced as [ə]
The first syllable unstressed	**a**way, **a**gree, **a**buse, **a**board, **a**gainst, **a**dvice, **a**ttain, **a**dvance, c**a**nal, c**o**rrect, p**o**lice, supp**o**rt
The second syllable unstressed	doct**or**, und**er**, fig**ure**, col**our**, abs**e**nt, const**a**nt, stand**ard**, **o**ral, forw**ard**, upw**ard**, awkw**ard**

A17
🎧 Unstressed positions

and	**a**	**an**
Fish **and** chips	Get **a** spoon	Have **an** apple
Salt **and** pepper	Cut **a** piece	**A** question **and an** answer
Pork **and** beans	Here's **a** plate	**An** aunt **and an** uncle
Ladies **and** gentlemen	Lend **a** hand	Listen to **an** announcement

NB: Schwa is the most-used sound in English. Very often, unstressed syllables and words in a sentence are pronounced with a schwa.

A18
🎧 Comparison: [ə] and [ɜ:]

[ə]	[ɜ:]
slog**a**n	g**ir**l
forw**ard**	w**or**d
awkw**ard**	th**ir**d
stand**ard**	**ear**n
upw**ard**	w**or**d
backw**ard**	w**or**k

A19
🎧 Sentences

Listen and repeat. Read each sentence aloud slowly at first, then as if you were telling it to someone in a natural way.

1. What **are** you doing in Lond**o**n? We **are** looking f**or a** hairdress**er**.
2. Is it made **of** glass? No, it's made **of** plastic.
3. What c**a**n I do? What h**a**s she done? What h**a**ve you done?
4. She h**a**d done it before she came here.
5. **A**mand**a**, phone call f**or** you!
6. The c**o**nduct**or o**f the orchestr**a** w**a**s **a**mazed t**o** see th**e** viol**a** play**er** drink **a** scotch **a**nd sod**a**.
7. Tell my sist**er A**mand**a** t**o** buy some bett**er** banan**a**s **a**s well **a**s p**o**tatoes **a**nd t**o**matoes.

23

A20
🎧 **Comparison:** stressed and unstressed vowel position

Stressed position	Unstressed position, pronounced with [ə]
What are you looking **at**? [æ]	Look **at** him.
What is it made **of**? [ɒ]	It's made **of** cotton.
Where do you come fr**o**m? [ɒ]	I come fr**o**m Paris.
Who is it f**or**? [ɔ:]	It's f**or** you.
W**ou**ldn't you agree? [ʊ]	I w**ou**ld say yes.
W**ere**n't you there? [ɜ:]	We w**ere** absent.
W**a**sn't he there? [ɒ]	Yes, he w**a**s sitting next to me.

A21
🎧 **Verses**

Listen and copy the intonation and voice modulation on the CD.

My jeal**ou**sy I can't express,
Their love they op**e**nly c**o**nfess;
Her shell-like **ear**s she does not close
T**o** their recit**a**l **o**f their woes.

Classes of words that have the neutral vowel shwa [ə]

1. Endings of names: **A**mand**a**, Barbar**a**, Olg**a**, S**a**manth**a**, Arth**ur**.

2. UK Counties ending in "shire" will have [ə] after "sh":, Derbysh**ire**, Oxfordsh**ire**, Yorksh**ire**, Leicestersh**ire**, Lancash**ire**.

3. Names of places ending in "mouth" will usually have [ə] after "m": Bournem**ou**th, Exm**ou**th, Dartm**ou**th, Portsm**ou**th, Plym**ou**th.

4. Names of places ending in "ford" will have [ə] after "f": Brent**ford**, Ox**ford**, Guild**ford**, Rom**ford**, Strat**ford**, Hert**ford**.

5. Contraction of "have" to [əv]: could**'ve**, should**'ve**, must**'ve**, might**'ve**.

6. Auxiliary verbs in unstressed position will often have [ə]: h**a**ve, h**a**s, h**a**d, w**ere**, w**a**s, **a**re, **a**m.

7. Articles, prepositions and particles in unstressed position will often have [ə]: **a**, th**e**, t**o**, **o**f, **a**s, f**o**r, fr**o**m.

Additional exercises:

A: *Write down 4 words with the target sound that you often use when speaking English. Practice these words, thinking about your lips, tongue and jaw positions for the target sound.*

1. _____ 3. _____

2. _____ 4. _____

B: *Write down 4 words with the target sound that you often hear on TV, radio or from your friends/colleagues. Practice these words, thinking about your lips, tongue and jaw positions for the target sound.*

1. _____ 3. _____

2. _____ 4. _____

Lesson 7: The [ɪ] sound as in "pit"

Speech organs position:
Jaw is nearly closed, lips slightly spread; the front of the tongue rises high in the front of the mouth.

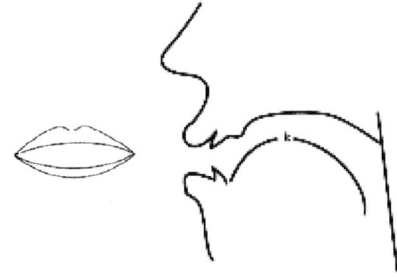

[ɪ   ɪ   ɪ]

A22
🎧 Words

Listen and repeat. Look at the mouth diagram to help you position your lips, tongue and jaw for the target sound.

Spelling variations for the [ɪ] sound	Highlighted bold letters pronounced as [ɪ]
i	h**i**m, h**i**larious, h**i**deous, h**i**nt, wh**i**m, v**i**sion, sp**i**rit
a	vill**a**ge, cabb**a**ge
e	d**e**lete, d**e**feat, d**e**lusion
y	cr**y**pt, s**y**non**y**m, s**y**mbol, s**y**mptoms, h**y**mn

A23
🎧 Sentences

Listen and repeat. Read each sentence aloud slowly at first, then as if you were telling it to someone in a natural way.

1. Those lett**u**ce**s** taste like cabb**a**ge**s**.
2. B**i**ll l**i**fted the l**i**d of the b**i**n tentatively and found not a s**i**ngle th**i**ng.
3. Tell J**i**ll I th**i**nk th**i**s **i**s a s**i**lly l**i**ttle game.
4. I can't stay a m**i**nute longer **i**n th**i**s m**i**serable l**i**ttle p**i**t!
5. T**i**m Gr**i**m **i**s a solid, respectable man and **i**s a p**i**llar of society.
6. Th**i**s s**i**mple th**i**ng, a wedd**i**ng r**i**ng, **i**s a s**y**mbol, th**e** oldest **i**n h**i**story.
7. Cl**i**mbing over a rocky mount**ai**n, sk**i**p the r**i**vulet and the fount**ai**n.

26

A24
🎧 Verses

Listen and copy the intonation and voice modulation on the CD.

Here's a first–rate opportunity
To get married with impunity,
To indulge in the felicity
Of unbounded domesticity.
You shall quickly be personified,
Conjugally matrimonified,
By a doctor of divinity,
Who resides in this vicinity.
(*W.S. Gilbert*)

Additional exercises:

A: *Write down 4 words with the target sound that you often use when speaking English. Practice these words, thinking about your lips, tongue and jaw positions for the target sound.*

1. _____ 3. _____

2. _____ 4. _____

B: *Write down 4 words with the target sound that you often hear on TV, radio or from your friends/colleagues. Practice these words, thinking about your lips, tongue and jaw positions for the target sound.*

1. _____ 3. _____

2. _____ 4. _____

Lesson 8: Comparison [ə] - [ɪ] and [ɪ] - [iː]

A25
🎧 **Letter:** 'e' in the article 'the' is pronounced as [ɪ] and [ə]

Letter 'e' is pronounced as [ɪ] in 'pit' (Lesson 7) when the next word begins with a vowel	Letter 'e' is pronounced as a schwa [ə] in 'the' (Lesson 6) when the next word begins with a consonant
th**e** **i**nstrument	th**e** **s**kill
th**e** **o**nly	th**e** **p**ill
th**e** **U**pper House	th**e** **s**hip
th**e** **o**dd	th**e** **p**itch
th**e** **e**nquiry	th**e** **k**itchen
th**e** **o**ak	th**e** **c**offin
th**e** **e**lision	th**e** **g**ymnast
th**e** **i**llness	th**e** **k**in

A26
🎧 **Comparison: long [iː] and short [ɪ]**

[ɪ]  [iː]

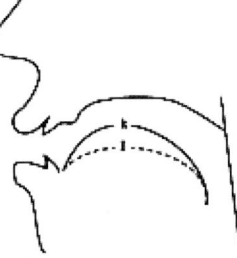

[iː]	[ɪ]	[iː]	[ɪ]
re**a**son	r**i**sen	b**ea**st	b**i**t
b**ee**n	b**i**n	q**uee**n	k**i**n
ease	**i**s	d**ea**l	d**i**ll
sl**ee**p	sl**i**p	n**ee**d	N**i**ck
ch**ea**p	ch**i**p	l**ee**k	l**y**ric
wh**ea**t	w**i**t	p**eo**ple	p**i**tch
l**ea**p	l**i**p	gr**ee**d	gr**i**d
f**ee**t	f**i**t	l**ea**ve	l**i**ve
t**ea**m	T**i**m	sn**ea**ky	sn**i**p

A27

🎧 **Words: long [iː] highlighted as bold and underlined and short [ɪ] highlighted as bold**

Listen and repeat. Look at the mouth diagram to help you position your lips, tongue and jaw for the target sound.

bel**ie**ve	gr**ea**sy	rel**ie**ve
rev**ea**l	**ea**sy	rep**ea**t
def**ea**t	sn**ee**zing	m**ee**ting
rec**e**de	th**e**sis	y**ie**lding
retr**ie**ve	s**ee**ing	s**ei**zing
rec**ei**pt	ser**e**ne	fr**ee**zing

A28

🎧 **Sentences: short [ɪ] highlighted as bold and long [iː] highlighted as bold and underlined**

Listen and repeat. Read each sentence aloud slowly at first, then as if you were telling it to someone in a natural way.

1. The w**i**dth of the sl**ee**ves st**i**ll n**ee**ds to f**i**t my n**ea**t l**i**nen jacket.
2. I am not particularly k**ee**n to g**i**ve the v**i**ctory to a d**i**fferent t**ea**m.
3. Th**e**se s**i**lver r**i**ngs belonged to Qu**ee**n **E**l**i**zabeth.
4. T**i**m **i**s compl**e**tely out of N**i**na's l**ea**gue and sh**e** **i**sn't k**ee**n on b**ei**ng chased by h**i**m.
5. There **i**s a l**i**ttle something m**i**ssing **i**n th**i**s m**ea**l. Have you tried to add some d**i**ll?
6. My next of k**i**n, **Mr. B**ea**n, **i**s a D**ea**n of L**ee**ds University.

A29
🎧 **Verses**

Listen and copy the intonation and voice modulation on the CD.

H**e** **i**s an **E**ngl**i**shman!
For h**e** h**i**mself has said **i**t,
And **i**t's greatl**y** to h**i**s credit,
That h**e** **i**s an **E**ngl**i**shman!

29

Additional exercises:

A: *Write down 4 words with the target sound that you often use when speaking English. Practice these words, thinking about your lips, tongue and jaw positions for the target sound.*

1. _____   3. _____

2. _____   4. _____

B: *Write down 4 words with the target sound that you often hear on TV, radio or from your friends/colleagues. Practice these words, thinking about your lips, tongue and jaw positions for the target sound.*

1. _____   3. _____

2. _____   4. _____

Lesson 9: The [ʌ] sound as in "hut"

Speech organs position:

The jaw is three quarters open, lips relaxed; the middle of the tongue rises slightly in the centre of the mouth.

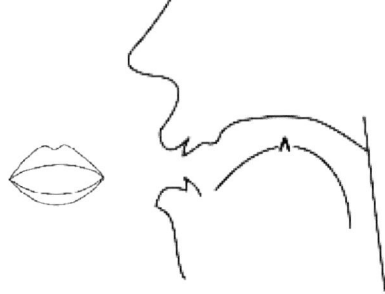

[ʌ   ʌ   ʌ]

A30
🎧 Words

Listen and repeat. Look at the mouth diagram to help you position your lips, tongue and jaw for the target sound.

Spelling variations for the [ʌ] sound	Highlighted bold letters pronounced as [ʌ]
u	m**u**st, l**u**ck, d**u**mp, j**u**st, **u**pper, n**u**n, b**u**s, l**u**nch
o	c**o**me, w**o**rry, fr**o**nt, l**o**ve, d**o**ne, **o**nce, c**o**ver
ou	r**ou**gh, t**ou**gh, c**ou**ntry, c**ou**ple, d**ou**ble, tr**ou**ble

A31
🎧 Sentences

Listen and repeat. Read each sentence aloud slowly at first, then as if you were telling it to someone in a natural way.

1. For s**o**me**o**ne with a l**o**ve of m**o**ney, the s**u**m of **o**ne h**u**ndred pounds was enticing.
2. B**u**d, l**o**ve! Don't w**o**rry; victory is in fr**o**nt of you!
3. I can't **u**nderstand the f**u**n of travelling by b**u**s on such r**ou**gh c**ou**ntry roads.
4. There are a n**u**mber of n**u**ns am**o**ng **u**s.
5. Here I am, in fr**o**nt of a t**u**b with a r**u**b and a scr**u**b!
6. When you c**o**me to l**u**nch in L**o**ndon on S**u**nday, remember to bring s**o**me m**o**ney.

A32
🎧 Word comparisons: [ɑː] and [ʌ] sounds

Listen and repeat. Look at the mouth diagram to help you position your lips, tongue and jaw for the target sound.

[ɑː]	[ʌ]
father	front
dark	duck
bath	bud
pardon	punch
startle	stuck
rather	rough
target	tough

A33
🎧 Verses

Listen and copy the intonation and voice modulation on the CD.

Your captain was the **o**ther!!!
They left their foster-m**o**ther,
The **o**ne was Ralph, our br**o**ther,
Our captain was the **o**ther,
A many years ago.

A many years ago two
tender babes I nursed!
One was of low condition,
The **o**ther **u**pper cr**u**st,
A regular patrician.
Oh, bitter is my c**u**p!
However could I do it?
I mixed those children **u**p...
(*W.S. Gilbert*)

33

Lesson 10: The [ɒ] sound as in "box"

Speech organs position:
The jaw is quite relaxed and open; the lips are coming forward a little. The back of the tongue rises slightly.

[ɒ   ɒ   ɒ]

A34
🎧 Words

Listen and repeat. Look at the mouth diagram to help you position your lips, tongue and jaw for the target sound.

Spelling variations for the [ɒ] sound	Highlighted bold letters pronounced as [ɒ]
o	fond, lock, stop, gone, odd, lost, sorry, wrong, often, clock, knock, obvious, promise, doctor
a	want, was, wander, wallet, wallow, wash, watch, warrior, waffle, squat, quantity

A35
🎧 Sentences

Listen and repeat. Read each sentence aloud slowly at first, then as if you were telling it to someone in a natural way.

1. A lot of odd documents in strong boxes are locked in the office.
2. Can I wash my cotton socks in the long pond?
3. The doctor promised to watch Tommy's cough and after four days the cough had stopped.
4. Sorry, I've forgotten my wallet in the shop.
5. The conversation in the office was moderated when the boss, Mr Oxford, came in.
6. Roger and Robin often spend their holidays in Scotland in October.

A36
🎧 Verses

Listen and copy the intonation and voice modulation on the CD.

All I want is a proper cup of coffee,
Made in a proper copper coffee pot.
Tin or iron coffee pots,
They're no use to me,
If I can't have a
Proper cup of coffee
In a proper copper coffee pot
I'll have a cup of tea.

Additional exercises:

A: *Write down 4 words with the target sound that you often use when speaking English. Practice these words, thinking about your lips, tongue and jaw positions for the target sound.*

1. _____ 3. _____

2. _____ 4. _____

B: *Write down 4 words with the target sound that you often hear on TV, radio or from your friends/colleagues. Practice these words, thinking about your lips, tongue and jaw positions for the target sound.*

1. _____ 3. _____

2. _____ 4. _____

Lesson 11: Comparison [ɒ] - [ɔː] and [ɒ] - [ʌ]

A37
🎧 **Word comparisons: long [ɔː] and short [ɒ]**

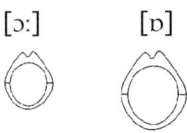

Listen and repeat. Look at the mouth diagram to help you position your lips, tongue and jaw for the target sound.

[ɔː]	[ɒ]	[ɔː]	[ɒ]
daughter	doll	portion	polish
lawn	lofty	gorgeous	gone
law	lobster	stalk	stock
morning	mock	naughty	notch
glorious	glossy	quarter	quality
bore	boss	ought	office
door	dog	walk	what

A38
🎧 **Word comparisons: [ʌ], [ɒ] and [ɔː] sounds**

Listen and repeat. Look at the mouth diagram to help you position your lips, tongue and jaw for the target sound.

[ʌ]	[ɒ]	[ɔː]
buddy	body	talk
tough	Chekhov	daughter
front	comment	orchestra
rough	economist	glorious
couple	politicians	ordinary

A39

🎧 Sentences: short [ɒ] highlighted as bold and long [ɔː] highlighted as black and underlined

Listen and repeat. Read each sentence aloud slowly at first, then as if you were telling it to someone in a natural way.

1. I have a l**o**t of l**o**ng and sh**or**t shirts.
2. I have b**ou**ght these **aw**esome ch**o**colates from the st**ore** at the t**o**p of Chekh**o**v Street in D**or**king.
3. T**o**m's n**au**ghty d**au**ghter ate **a**ll the l**o**bsters and str**aw**berries.
4. There was a gl**o**rious picture of **A**lmighty G**o**d on the w**a**ll in the c**o**ttage.
5. M**au**d's mind was c**au**ght with h**o**rrible d**au**nting th**ou**ghts.
6. Wh**a**t a g**or**geous g**o**lf c**our**se! T**o**p n**o**tch!
7. It doesn't b**ore** T**o**m to w**a**lk his d**o**g in the gl**o**rious **au**tumn m**or**ning.

Additional exercises:

A: *Write down 4 words with the target sounds that you often use when speaking English. Practice these words, thinking about your lips, tongue and jaw positions for the target sound.*

1. _____ 3. _____

2. _____ 4. _____

B: *Write down 4 words with the target sounds that you often hear on TV, radio or from your friends/colleagues. Practice these words, thinking about your lips, tongue and jaw positions for the target sound.*

1. _____ 3. _____

2. _____ 4. _____

Lesson 12: The [e] sound as in "pet"

Speech organs position:
Jaw is half open, lips are
in a soft smile position;
the front of the tongue rises
three quarters of the way up
towards the roof of the mouth.

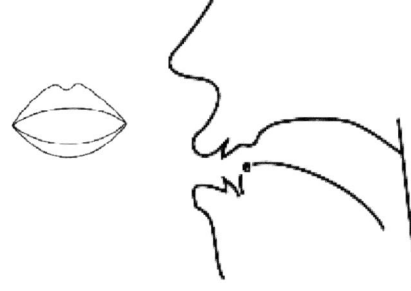

[e   e   e]

A40
🎧 **Words**

Listen and repeat. Look at the mouth diagram to help you position your lips, tongue and jaw for the target sound.

Spelling variations for the [e] sound	Highlighted bold letters pronounced as [e]
e	s**e**nsible, wr**e**n, b**e**g, b**e**nt, g**e**ntle, g**e**nerosity
eo	l**eo**pard, j**eo**pardy
ea	h**ea**d, w**ea**lth, m**ea**sure, pl**ea**sure, thr**ea**d, l**ea**ther
ei	l**ei**sure, L**ei**cester, fri**e**nd
ay	s**ay**s

A41
🎧 **Comparison:** [ə] and [e]

[ə]	[e]
c**a**nal	k**e**nnel
c**o**rrect	k**e**pt
g**a**zette	g**e**ld
p**o**lice	p**e**nce
s**u**pport	s**e**lf-help
c**o**mmand	k**e**tchup
American	**e**mbassy

38

A42
🎧 Sentences

Listen and repeat. Read each sentence aloud slowly at first, then as if you were telling it to someone in a natural way.

1. "It's best for your pet's health to rest", said an educated vet to a wealthy gentlemen.
2. Educated men have always measured every word they said.
3. Twenty-seven shepherds hesitated before entering the sheep-pen.
4. It's a real pleasure to rest on a nice leather sofa.
5. A red leather jacket was well presented on the display.
6. The weather was wet and windy when the men were mending the fence.

A43
🎧 Verses

Listen and copy the intonation and voice modulation on the CD.

Let us gaily tread the measure,
Make the most of fleeting leisure;
Every moment brings a treasure,
Of its own especial pleasure...
Let us gaily tread the measure.

Additional exercises:

A: *Write down 4 words with the target sound that you often use when speaking English. Practice these words, thinking about your lips, tongue and jaw positions for the target sound.*

1. _____ 3. _____

2. _____ 4. _____

B: *Write down 4 words with the target sound that you often hear on TV, radio or from your friends/colleagues. Practice these words, thinking about your lips, tongue and jaw positions for the target sound.*

1. _____ 3. _____

2. _____ 4. _____

Lesson 13: The [ʊ] sound as in "book"

Speech organs position:
The jaw is almost closed,
lips rounded and forward.
The back of the tongue is high
in the back of the mouth.

[ʊ   ʊ   ʊ]

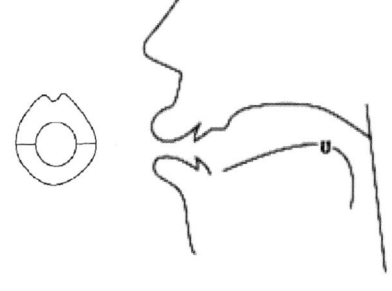

A44
🎧 Words

Listen and repeat. Look at the mouth diagram to help you position your lips, tongue and jaw for the target sound.

Spelling variations for the [ʊ] sound	Highlighted bold letters pronounced as [ʊ]
u	p**u**t, p**u**sh, f**u**ll, b**u**tcher, spoonf**u**l, fulf**i**l, c**u**shion
oo, o	b**oo**k, l**oo**k, g**oo**d, w**oo**l, w**oo**d, w**o**lf, f**oo**t, st**oo**d
oul	c**ou**ld, w**ou**ld, sh**ou**ld

A45
🎧 Sentences

Listen and repeat. Read each sentence aloud slowly at first, then as if you were telling it to someone in a natural way.

1. Could you put this good Worcester wool in the wooden chest?
2. The butcher saw a wolf looking in every nook for the fallen rook.
3. Our cook couldn't cook without looking at his cookery book.
4. If I could just get off the hook and get rid of my responsibility to cook.
5. You could easily lose your foothold in the bulrushes by the brook on the way to the "Bull and Bush" pub.
6. If you are preparing a pudding you must have sugar and a good cookery book.

40

A46
🎧 **Verses**

Listen and copy the intonation and voice modulation on the CD.

W**ou**ld you take this b**oo**k!
C**ou**ld you leave that h**oo**k!
Let us walk by f**oo**t!
That sounds g**oo**d!
We c**ou**ld, we w**ou**ld, we sh**ou**ld!

Additional exercises:

A: *Write down 4 words with the target sound that you often use when speaking English. Practice these words, thinking about your lips, tongue and jaw positions for the target sound.*

1. _____ 3. _____

2. _____ 4. _____

B: *Write down 4 words with the target sound that you often hear on TV, radio or from your friends/colleagues. Practice these words, thinking about your lips, tongue and jaw positions for the target sound.*

1. _____ 3. _____

2. _____ 4. _____

Lesson 14: Comparison [ʊ] and [uː]

A47

🎧 **Contrast between short** [ʊ] **and long** [uː]

[ʊ] [uː]

[ʊ]	[uː]	[ʊ]	[uː]
could	clue	good	glued
foot	food	wood	wound
full	fruit	book	boom
look	loose	took	true
put	pool	rook	rouge
should	shoes	soot	soon

A48

🎧 **Sentences: short** [ʊ] **sound highlighted as bold and long** [uː] **highlighted as black and underlined**

Listen and repeat. Read each sentence aloud slowly at first, then as if you were telling it to someone in a natural way.

1. The w**ou**nded w**o**lf c**ou**ldn't m**o**ve his f**oo**t and s**oo**n fell asleep under the b**u**sh.
2. W**o**rcester w**oo**l w**ou**ld s**ui**t b**eau**tifully for my n**ew** bl**ue** s**ui**t.
3. Natural f**oo**ds contrib**u**te to a g**oo**d diet.
4. Behaving l**oo**sely c**ou**ld be seen as f**oo**lish and w**ou**ldn't impr**o**ve your l**oo**k.
5. G**oo**d b**oo**ks **u**sually f**u**lfil people's lives.

Additional exercises:

A: *Write down 4 words with the target sound that you often use when speaking English. Practice these words, thinking about your lips, tongue and jaw positions for the target sound.*

1. _____ 3. _____

2. _____ 4. _____

B: *Write down 4 words with the target sound that you often hear on TV, radio or from your friends/colleagues. Practice these words, thinking about your lips, tongue and jaw positions for the target sound.*

1. _____ 3. _____

2. _____ 4. _____

Lesson 15: The [æ] sound as in "mad"

Speech organs position:
Open jaw, open loose lips;
tongue almost flat at the
bottom of the mouth.
The sound is made in the front
of the mouth.

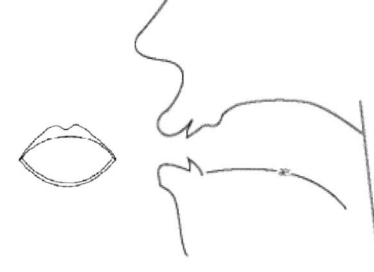

[æ   æ   æ]

A49
🎧 Words

Listen and repeat. Look at the mouth diagram to help you position your lips, tongue and jaw for the target sound.

Japanese, barrage, nationalities, bad, happened, land, understand, activity, prank, miraculous, panther, ragged, man, actually

A50
🎧 Comparison: [e] and [æ] sounds

[e]	[æ]	[e]	[æ]
men	man	beg	bag
guessed	gassed	pet	pat
fed	fad	ten	tan
hem	ham	said	sad
hetero	hand	breath	bandage
wren	rank	kettle	candle

A51
🎧 Comparison: [ə], [e] and [æ]

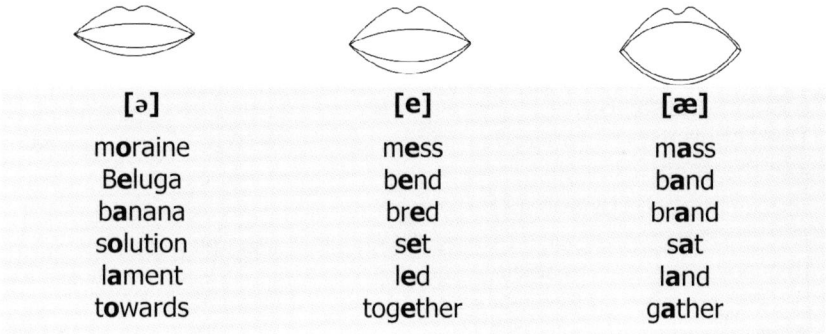

[ə]	[e]	[æ]
moraine	mess	mass
Beluga	bend	band
banana	bred	brand
solution	set	sat
lament	led	land
towards	together	gather

A52
🎧 Sentences

Listen and repeat. Read each sentence aloud slowly at first, then as if you were telling it to someone in a natural way.

1. A black fat cat was sad when he couldn't grab a slice of ham.
2. It can be quite a challenge to manage a marriage.
3. A man who looked unhappy sang a sad bad mad romantic song.
4. As a habit I add some tomato to my hamburger.
5. Standing hand in hand, the man asked Jan for her hand in marriage.
6. Can you manage to carry those magazines back to the rack?

A53
🎧 Verses

Listen and copy the intonation and voice modulation on the CD.

What was that?
It was the cat!

Pull ashore in fashion steady,
For the clergyman is ready
To unite the happy pair!
(*W.S. Gilbert*)

45

Lesson 16: Diphthong [əʊ] as in "boat"

Speech organs position:

Start with relaxed lips and
tongue in [ə] as in "the"
position (Lesson 6).
Then bring the lips forward
into the short [ʊ] as in
"book" position (Lesson 13).

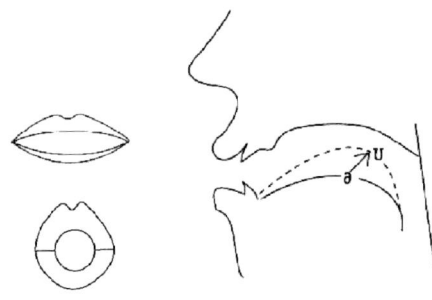

[ə ə əʊ   ə ə əʊ   əʊ əʊ əʊ]

A54
🎧 Words

Listen and repeat. Look at the mouth diagram to help you position your lips, tongue and jaw for the target sound.

Spelling variations for the [əʊ] sound	Highlighted bold letters pronounced as [əʊ]
o	h**o**pe, r**o**le, f**o**cus, th**o**se, b**o**th, cl**o**thes, b**o**ld, **o**pen, wh**o**le
oa	r**oa**d, **oa**k, c**oa**t
ow	gl**ow**, sorr**ow**, pill**ow**, foll**ow**, sparr**ow**, thr**ow**
ew	s**ew**

A55
🎧 Sentences

Listen and repeat. Read each sentence aloud slowly at first, then as if you were telling it to someone in a natural way.

1. **Jo**an has a c**o**ld in her n**o**se because she r**o**de her p**o**ny through the fr**o**zen sn**ow**.
2. The p**o**etry of b**o**ld p**o**ems imp**o**sed a strange t**o**ne on the wh**o**le sh**ow**.
3. I d**o**n't kn**ow** when I will come h**o**me, although I am cl**o**sely f**o**cusing on the r**oa**d. But soon, m**o**st probably, I will kn**ow** and will ph**o**ne you as I come cl**o**ser to our h**o**me.
4. When speaking on the p**o**dium keep your sh**ou**lders **o**pen!

46

5. Discharge your **loa**thsome **loa**ds! Belch forth your venom, **toa**ds!
6. **Joe**, d**o**n't g**o** to **O**klah**o**ma or **O**hi**o** but come h**o**me to R**o**me instead.

A56
🎧 Verses

Listen and copy the intonation and voice modulation on the CD.

M**o**ses supp**o**ses his t**oe**ses are r**o**ses,
But M**o**ses supp**o**ses err**o**neously;
For n**o**body's t**oe**ses are p**o**sies of r**o**ses
As M**o**ses supp**o**ses his t**oe**ses to be.

Additional exercises:

A: *Write down 4 words with the target sound that you often use when speaking English. Practice these words, thinking about your lips, tongue and jaw positions for the target sound.*

1. _____ 3. _____

2. _____ 4. _____

B: *Write down 4 words with the target sound that you often hear on TV, radio or from your friends/colleagues. Practice these words, thinking about your lips, tongue and jaw positions for the target sound.*

1. _____ 3. _____

2. _____ 4. _____

Lesson 17: Diphthong [eɪ] as in "pay"

Speech organs position:
Start in [e] as in "pet" position,
with the lips in a soft smile and
raised front of the tongue
(Lesson 12).
Then the front of the tongue rises
a little more forward, to [ɪ] as in
"pit" position, and the lips spread
slightly (Lesson 7).

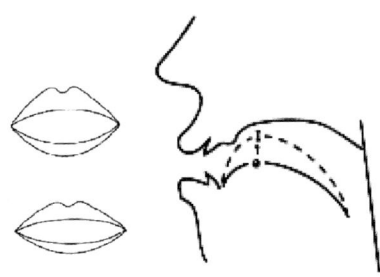

[e e eɪ   e e eɪ   eɪ eɪ eɪ]

A57
🎧 Words

Listen and repeat. Look at the mouth diagram to help you position your lips, tongue and jaw for the target sound.

Spelling variations for the [eɪ] sound	Highlighted bold letters pronounced as [eɪ]
a	t**a**ke, arr**a**nge, l**a**te, t**a**pe, am**a**ze, ch**a**nge, sh**a**pe, stimul**a**te, popul**a**te
ai	**ai**m, r**ai**nbow, v**ai**n, g**ai**n, pl**ai**n
ay	p**ay**, g**ay**, tr**ay**, betr**ay**
eigh, aigh	w**eigh**t, **eigh**t, str**aigh**t

A58
🎧 Sentences

Listen and repeat. Read each sentence aloud slowly at first, then as if you were telling it to someone in a natural way.

1. The tr**ai**n at **eigh**t was very l**a**te; we left the st**a**tion with frustr**a**tion.
2. Betr**ay**ed and am**a**zed we **ai**med h**a**stily for the Ch**ai**n Walk brasserie.
3. We p**a**tiently w**ai**ted in v**ai**n for our f**a**vourite t**a**ble to become v**a**cant.
4. To n**a**me your child with an **a**ncient

name some m**ay** consider ins**a**ne!
5. All the f**a**vourite c**a**kes that J**a**ne had m**a**de were pl**a**ced on tr**ay**s.
6. You must p**ay** any d**ay** if you are going aw**ay** on the tr**ai**n.

A59
🎧 Verses

Instructions: Copy the intonation and modulate the voice after the CD.

St**ay**, Frederic, st**ay**!
They have no legal cl**ai**m,
No shadow of a sh**a**me
Will fall upon my n**a**me.

Additional exercises:

A: *Write down 4 words with the target sound that you often use when speaking English. Practice these words, thinking about your lips, tongue and jaw positions for the target sound.*

1. _____ 3. _____

2. _____ 4. _____

B: *Write down 4 words with the target sound that you often hear on TV, radio or from your friends/colleagues. Practice these words, thinking about your lips, tongue and jaw positions for the target sound.*

1. _____ 3. _____

2. _____ 4. _____

Lesson 18: Diphthong [ɔɪ] as in "boy"

Speech organs position:

Start in [ɔ:] as in "fort"
position, lips forward and quite
tight; the jaw is fairly
closed (Lesson 3).
Then move to [ɪ] as in "pit"
position; the tongue rises forward,
lips slightly spread (Lesson 12).

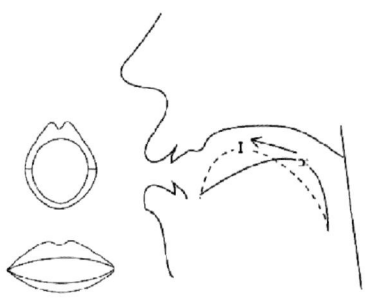

[ɔ: ɔ: ɔɪ   ɔ: ɔ: ɔɪ   ɔɪ ɔɪ ɔɪ]

A60
🎧 Words

Listen and repeat. Look at the mouth diagram to help you position your lips, tongue and jaw for the target sound.

Spelling variations for the [ɔɪ] sound	Highlighted bold letters pronounced as [ɔɪ]
oi	c**oi**n, expl**oi**t, m**oi**sture, b**oi**l, sp**oi**l, p**oi**se, an**oi**nt, s**oi**l, p**oi**nts, br**oi**l, f**oi**l, l**oi**ter
oy	enj**oy**, l**oy**al, ann**oy**, r**oy**al, t**oy**, Ll**oy**d, dec**oy**, destr**oy**

A61
🎧 Sentences

Listen and repeat. Read each sentence aloud slowly at first, then as if you were telling it to someone in a natural way.

1. Tr**oy** was once destr**oy**ed by flamb**oy**ant n**oi**sy soldiers.
2. A n**oi**sy v**oi**ce can be so ann**oy**ing that the whole image can be sp**oi**led.
3. Rice requires m**oi**st s**oi**l and months of t**oi**l.
4. Any n**oi**se ann**oy**s an **oy**ster, but a n**oi**sy n**oi**se ann**oy**s an **oy**ster most.
5. You can't enj**oy** the beef if the j**oi**nt is covered with b**oi**ling **oi**l.
6. M**oi**ra was very ann**oy**ed at the b**oi**sterous n**oi**se of her t**oy**-b**oy** enj**oy**ing his **oy**sters.

A62
🎧 Verses

Listen and copy the intonation and voice modulation on the CD.

An orphan b**oy**,
Forgo your cruel empl**oy**,
How sad – an orphan b**oy**.
If pity you can feel,
Leave me my sole remaining j**oy** –
Against the sad, sad tale of the lonely orphan b**oy**!
(*W.S. Gilbert*)

Additional exercises

A: *Write down 4 words with the target sound that you often use when speaking English. Practice these words, thinking about your lips, tongue and jaw positions for the target sound.*

1. _____   3. _____

2. _____   4. _____

B: *Write down 4 words with the target sound that you often hear on TV, radio or from your friends/colleagues. Practice these words, thinking about your lips, tongue and jaw positions for the target sound.*

1. _____   3. _____

2. _____   4. _____

Lesson 19: Diphthong [ɪə] as in "hear"

Speech organs position:
Start with the tongue high in
the front of the mouth in
[ɪ] position as in the "pit"
position (Lesson 7).
Then drop the tongue back
into [ə] position as in the
"the" position (Lesson 6).

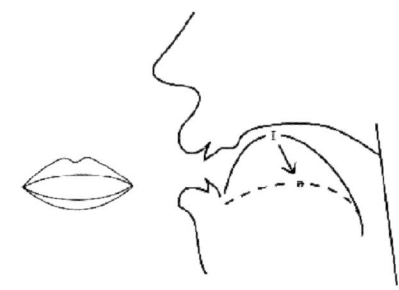

[ɪ ɪ ɪə   ɪ ɪ ɪə   ɪə ɪə ɪə]

A63
🎧 Words

Listen and repeat. Look at the mouth diagram to help you position your lips, tongue and jaw for the target sound.

Spelling variations for the [ɪə] sound	Highlighted bold letters pronounced as [ɪə]
ea	cer**ea**l, nucl**ea**r, g**ea**r, n**ea**rly, th**ea**tre
ie	exper**ie**nce, b**ie**r, p**ie**r, caval**ie**r
io	super**io**r, exter**io**r
iou	myster**iou**s, cur**iou**s, spur**iou**s
ei	w**ei**rd, w**ei**r
er	sph**er**e, interf**er**e, h**er**e, qu**ee**r, p**ee**r, sh**ee**r

A64
🎧 Sentences

Listen and repeat. Read each sentence aloud slowly at first, then as if you were telling it to someone in a natural way.

1. V**er**a, d**ea**r, wipe your t**ea**rs, come n**ea**r h**er**e and forget your f**ea**r!
2. My exper**ie**nce of p**ie**rcing V**er**a's **ea**rs was rather w**ei**rd.
3. R**ea**lly d**ea**r b**ee**r makes me ch**ee**rful but spur**iou**s b**ee**r makes me fur**iou**s.
4. It was qu**ee**r to exper**ie**nce a y**ea**r with my caval**ie**r p**ee**rs at L**ea**r's.

52

5. Last **yea**r I had a deli**rio**us expe**rie**nce when I was allowed to st**eer** the boat n**ear** the w**eir**.
6. My t**ear**fulness soon cl**ear**ed when I met the d**ear**, f**ear**less, myster**iou**s stranger.

A65
🎧 **Verses**

Listen and copy the intonation and voice modulation on the CD.

Sad is that woman's lot who, **year** by **year**,
Sees, one by one, her beauties disapp**ear**,
When Time, grown w**ea**ry of her heart-
drawn sighs,
Impatiently begins to 'dim her eyes'!

Additional exercises:

A: *Write down 4 words with the target sound that you often use when speaking English. Practice these words, thinking about your lips, tongue and jaw positions for the target sound.*

1. _____ 3. _____

2. _____ 4. _____

B: *Write down 4 words with the target sound that you often hear on TV, radio or from your friends/colleagues. Practice these words, thinking about your lips, tongue and jaw positions for the target sound.*

1. _____ 3. _____

2. _____ 4. _____

Lesson 20: Diphthong [aɪ] as in "pie"

Speech organs position:
Start with flat tongue, open
jaw in [a] position as in "pasta".
Then move to [ɪ] as in "pit"
position; the jaw closes, the
tongue rises, lips slightly spread
(Lesson 12).

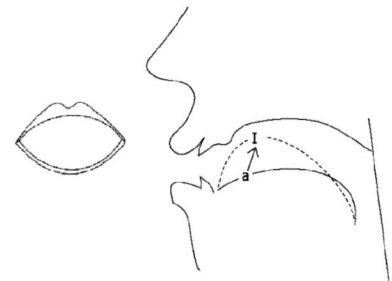

[a a aɪ   a a aɪ   aɪ aɪ aɪ]

A66
🎧 Words

Listen and repeat. Look at the mouth diagram to help you position your lips, tongue and jaw for the target sound.

Spelling variations for the [aɪ] sound	Highlighted bold letters pronounced as [aɪ]
y	sk**y**, fl**y**, cr**y**, suppl**y**, terrif**y**, den**y**
i	**i**dle, sl**i**de, sh**i**ne, w**i**ld, advert**i**se, des**i**gn, m**i**nd
igh	m**igh**t, h**igh**, n**igh**, del**igh**t, r**igh**t
ui	q**ui**te, g**ui**de

A67
🎧 Sentences

Listen and repeat. Read each sentence aloud slowly at first, then as if you were telling it to someone in a natural way.

1. Tr**y** to find a br**igh**t **i**dea behind the rh**y**mes of Oscar Wilde.
2. The sun is no longer h**igh** in the sk**y** as the day declines.
3. "His wife is q**ui**te mild and kind." What? Are you blind?
4. There are some g**uy**s in St. **I**ves who have up to seven wives.
5. Holding their chins q**ui**te h**igh** nine kn**igh**ts were riding by.
6. Tr**y** not to be frightened of spiders, just hide when they come in s**igh**t – they won't bite!
7. Nine men with fine tenor voices decided to sing q**ui**te h**igh** in the choir on Friday night.

A68
🎧 Verses

Listen and copy the intonation and voice modulation on the CD.

There was a lady loved a swine,
She kindly asked:
Pig-hog will you be mine?
I will build you a silver sty,
In which you will idly lie.

Additional exercises:

A: *Write down 4 words with the target sound that you often use when speaking English. Practice these words, thinking about your lips, tongue and jaw positions for the target sound.*

1. _____ 3. _____

2. _____ 4. _____

B: *Write down 4 words with the target sound that you often hear on TV, radio or from your friends/colleagues. Practice these words, thinking about your lips, tongue and jaw positions for the target sound.*

1. _____ 3. _____

2. _____ 4. _____

Lesson 21: Diphthong [ʊə] as in "sewer, triphthong [jʊə] as in "fewer"

Speech organs position:

Start with lips forward in the
[ʊ] position as in "book"
(Lesson 13).
Then move to [ə] position,
as in "the", with the lips falling
back and jaw opening.
(Lesson 6).

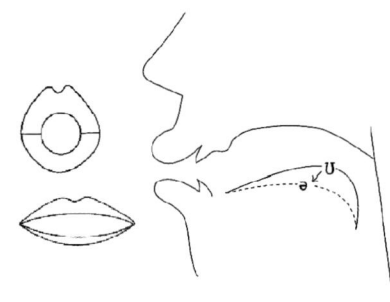

[ʊ ʊ ʊə   ʊ ʊ ʊə   ʊə ʊə ʊə]

A69
🎧 Words

Listen and repeat. Look at the mouth diagram to help you position your lips, tongue and jaw for the target sound.

Spelling variations for the [ʊə] sound	Highlighted bold letters pronounced as [ʊə]
or	p**oor**, m**oor**, t**our**, j**ur**y, cas**ua**l, l**ur**e, d**our**
ur	ins**ur**e, r**ur**al, ass**ur**e, Dr**ur**y, pl**ur**al
ew	s**ew**er, j**ew**el, br**ew**er
Spelling variations for the [jʊə] sound	Highlighted bold letters pronounced as [jʊə]
ur	man**ur**e, p**ur**e, mat**ur**e, obsc**ur**e
ua	d**ua**l, f**ue**l, man**ua**l
we	f**ew**er

A70
🎧 Sentences

Listen and repeat. Read each sentence aloud slowly at first, then as if you were telling it to someone in a natural way.

1. The immat**ur**e j**ur**y was uns**ur**e and could no longer end**ur**e sp**ur**ious ass**ur**ances.
2. Obsc**ur**e r**ur**al m**oor**s all**ur**e M**ur**iel more than lux**ur**ious j**ew**els.
3. D**our** Mr. R**uhr** was end**ur**ing the c**ur**e after his fiasco in am**our**.
4. The p**ur**e girl was l**ur**ed into the s**ew**ers by the f**ur**ious stew**ar**d.

5. I ass**ur**e you, the r**ur**al Yorkshire m**oo**rs are worth visiting on your to**ur** of E**ur**ope.

A71
🎧 Verses

Listen and copy the intonation and voice modulation on the CD.

False is he whose vows all**ur**ing
Make the listening echoes ring;
Sweet and low when all-end**ur**ing
Are the songs the lovers sing!

Additional exercises:

A: *Write down 4 words with the target sound that you often use when speaking English. Practice these words, thinking about your lips, tongue and jaw positions for the target sound.*

1. _____ 3. _____

2. _____ 4. _____

B: *Write down 4 words with the target sound that you often hear on TV, radio or from your friends/colleagues. Practice these words, thinking about your lips, tongue and jaw positions for the target sound.*

1. _____ 3. _____

2. _____ 4. _____

Lesson 22: Diphthong [eə] as in "pair"

Speech organs position:

Start in [e] as in "pet" position,
lips spread, front of the tongue
lifted in the front of the mouth
(Lesson 12).
Then the tongue relaxes back
into [ə] as in "the" position;
the lips become floppy and loose
(Lesson 6).

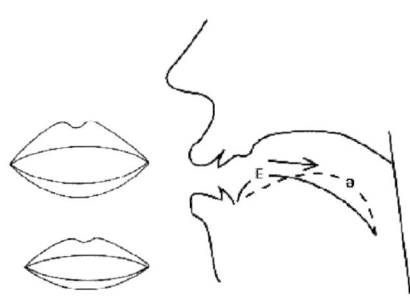

[e e eə   e e eə   eə eə eə]

A72
🎧 Words

Listen and repeat. Look at the mouth diagram to help you position your lips, tongue and jaw for the target sound.

Spelling variations for the [eə] sound	Highlighted bold letters pronounced as [eə]
air	rep**air**, f**air**y, desp**air**, fl**air**, m**ayor**, p**ear**
a before **r**	prec**ar**ious, sc**ar**cely, vic**ar**ious, nef**ar**ious, c**are**
are	sc**are**s, squ**are**, c**are**less, comp**are**, bew**are**, gl**are**

A73
🎧 Sentences

Listen and repeat. Read each sentence aloud slowly at first, then as if you were telling it to someone in a natural way.

1. Please, take c**are** of our h**eir**! But bew**are**, he can be unb**ear**able.
2. I comp**are**d my questionn**aire** with Cl**are**'s and fell into desp**air** as I become aw**are** that my questionn**aire** was rather b**are**.
3. I cannot d**are** nor be able to b**ear** an aff**air** with a married man.
4. I like to w**ear** my h**air** groomed with c**are**.
5. I'm prep**are**d to sw**ear** that the M**ayor** r**are**ly sh**are**d a h**are**.
6. Take c**are**! These ch**air**s have had th**eir** f**air** share of w**ear** and t**ear**.

A74
🎧 Verses

Listen and copy the intonation and voice modulation on the CD.

Oh! Chancellor unw**ary**,
Your attitude is v**ar**y!
Your badinage so **air**y,
Your manner arbitr**ar**y,
Are out of place
When face to face
With an influential F**air**y.
(*W.S. Gilbert*)

Additional exercises:

A: *Write down 4 words with the target sound that you often use when speaking English. Practice these words, thinking about your lips, tongue and jaw positions for the target sound.*

1. _____ 3. _____

2. _____ 4. _____

B: *Write down 4 words with the target sound that you often hear on TV, radio or from your friends/colleagues. Practice these words, thinking about your lips, tongue and jaw positions for the target sound.*

1. _____ 3. _____

2. _____ 4. _____

Lesson 23: Diphthong [aʊ] as in "how"

Speech organs position:
Start with flat tongue, open jaw in [a] position as in "pasta". Then bring the lips forward into the short [ʊ] position as in "book" (Lesson 13).

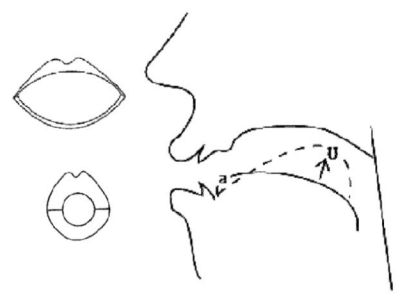

[a a aʊ   a a aʊ   aʊ aʊ aʊ]

A75
🎧 Words

Listen and repeat. Look at the mouth diagram to help you position your lips, tongue and jaw for the target sound.

Spelling variations for the [aʊ] sound	Highlighted bold letters pronounced as [aʊ]
ou	f**ou**nd, m**ou**se, spr**ou**t, b**ou**nce, sh**ou**t, l**ou**d, d**ou**bt, sc**ou**t, m**ou**ntain, th**ou**sand, f**ou**ntain
ow	pr**ow**, tr**ow**el, v**ow**el, **ow**l, n**ow**, end**ow**, fl**ow**er

A76
🎧 Sentences

Listen and repeat. Read each sentence aloud slowly at first, then as if you were telling it to someone in a natural way.

1. No d**ou**bt we can find th**ou**sands of fl**ow**ers in the Swiss m**ou**ntains.
2. H**ow** n**ow** br**ow**n c**ow**.
3. I saw a cl**ow**n sh**ou**ting in the t**ow**n.
4. Here lies the body of Jonathan P**ou**nd who was last seen at sea and never f**ou**nd.
5. The l**ou**d s**ou**nd of the h**ou**nds conf**ou**nded the br**ow**n m**ou**se.
6. With a sh**ou**t, the boy f**ou**nd a th**ou**sand p**ou**nds to the s**ou**th of the t**ow**n.

A77
🎧 Verses

Listen and copy the intonation and voice modulation on the CD.

Teddy worried ab**ou**t
The fact that he was rather st**ou**t.
But now he is pr**ou**d of being short and st**ou**t.

Additional exercises:

A: *Write down 4 words with the target sound that you often use when speaking English. Practice these words, thinking about your lips, tongue and jaw positions for the target sound.*

1. _____   3. _____

2. _____   4. _____

B: *Write down 4 words with the target sound that you often hear on TV, radio or from your friends/colleagues. Practice these words, thinking about your lips, tongue and jaw positions for the target sound.*

1. _____   3. _____

2. _____   4. _____

Lesson 24: Semi-vowel [j] as in "yes"

Semi-vowels: start in the position of one vowel and immediately move to another vowel.

Speech organs position:
Start with the front of the tongue high as in [iː] "feet"; then, immediately move the tongue down to the neutral [ə] schwa position.

[j   j   j]

B1
🎧 Words

Listen and repeat. Look at the mouth diagram to help you position your lips, tongue and jaw for the target sound.

Spelling variations for the [j] sound	Highlighted bold letters pronounced as [j]
y	**y**oung, **y**es, **y**ou, **y**esterday, **y**ard, **y**arn
u	**u**se, arg**u**e, val**u**e, d**u**ty, h**u**ge, ass**u**me, ref**u**se, conf**u**se, **u**nisex
ew	n**ew**, f**ew**er

B2
🎧 Sentences

Listen and repeat. Read each sentence aloud slowly at first, then as if you were telling it to someone in a natural way.

1. **Y**esterday, we had to q**u**eue to get into K**ew**.
2. I ref**u**se to arg**u**e with **y**ou. Exc**u**se me, I have d**u**ties to purs**u**e.
3. I was conf**u**sed that the bank ref**u**sed to accept my **Eu**ros.
4. The **y**outh **y**elled out, "I **y**earn to go to **Y**ork!"
5. **Y**ou kn**ew** **y**esterday's n**ew**s about the **Eu**ropean **y**achts tour, didn't **y**ou?
6. In the **Eu**ropean **U**nion, the sound of b**eau**tiful m**u**sic is not **u**nique.

B3
🎧 **Verses**

Listen and copy the intonation and voice modulation on the CD.

Love that no wrong can c**u**re,
Love that is always n**ew**,
Love that will aye end**u**re,
Though the rewards be f**ew**,
That is the love that's p**u**re,
That is the love that's true!

Additional exercises:

A: *Write down 4 words with the target sound that you often use when speaking English. Practice these words, thinking about your lips, tongue and jaw positions for the target sound.*

1. _____   3. _____

2. _____   4. _____

B: *Write down 4 words with the target sound that you often hear on TV, radio or from your friends/colleagues. Practice these words, thinking about your lips, tongue and jaw positions for the target sound.*

1. _____   3. _____

2. _____   4. _____

Lesson 25: Semi-vowel [w] as in "was"

Speech organs position:
Start with the lips forward,
as in [uː] "boot", then
immediately pull the lips back
to the neutral [ə] schwa position.

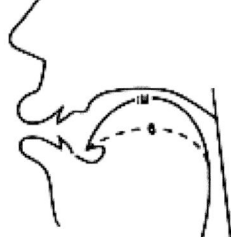

B4

🎧 **Repeat once from left to right:**

w	w	w	w
ww	ww	ww	w
www	www	www	w
wwww	wwww	wwww	w

B5

🎧 **Repeat each line four times:**

1. **W**ill you?
2. **W**ill you **w**ait?
3. **W**ill you **w**ait for **W**illy?
4. **W**ill you **w**ait for **W**illy and **W**innie?
5. **W**ill you **w**ait for **W**illy and **W**innie **W**illiams?

B6
🎧 Words

Listen and repeat. Look at the mouth diagram to help you position your lips, tongue and jaw for the target sound.

Spelling variations for the [w] sound	Highlighted bold letters pronounced as [w]
w	**w**ax, **w**olf, **w**ork, **w**ait, **w**ant, **w**atch, **w**eather
wh	**wh**ale, **wh**eel, **wh**ether
u after **q**	q**u**een, q**u**ench, q**u**antity
o	**o**nce, some**o**ne

B7
🎧 Words: contrasts with [v] and [w]

Listen and repeat. Look at the mouth diagram to help you position your lips, tongue and jaw for the target sound.

[v]	**[w]**	[v]	**[w]**
vet	**w**et	veal	**wh**eel
vest	**w**est	vend	**w**end
vale	**wh**ale	vent	**w**ent
vain	**w**ane	verse	**w**orse
via	**w**ire	vile	**wh**ile
vine	**w**ine	vim	**wh**im

B8
🎧 Sentences

Listen and repeat. Read each sentence aloud slowly at first, then as if you were telling it to someone in a natural way.

1. **W**ill you be req**ui**red to **w**ork in **W**estw**o**od on **W**ednesdays?
2. I **w**ondered **wh**ether any **o**ne of you **w**ere **w**illing to acq**ui**re our exq**ui**site **w**ines.
3. The q**ua**litative results **w**ere not **w**hat **w**e **w**anted from our q**ua**ntifiable q**ue**stionnaire q**ue**stions.
4. Every**o**ne **w**ould **w**ant to have as a **w**ife a **w**ondrous **w**ise **w**oman **w**ith beautiful eyes.
5. A **W**elshman in **w**ellington boots **w**andered into the **w**oods **w**ith his cool dudes.

6. He **w**on the a**w**ard for having **w**orn the **w**orld's **w**orst **w**orsted **w**aistcoat.

B9
🎧 Verses

Instructions: Copy the intonation and modulate the voice after the CD.

We are blind, and **w**e **w**ould see;
We are bound, and **w**e **w**ould be free;
We are dumb, and **w**e **w**ould talk;
We are lame, and **w**e **w**ould **w**alk.

Additional exercises:

A: *Write down 4 words with the target sound that you often use when speaking English. Practice these words, thinking about your lips, tongue and jaw positions for the target sound.*

1. _____ 3. _____

2. _____ 4. _____

B: *Write down 4 words with the target sound that you often hear on TV, radio or from your friends/colleagues. Practice these words, thinking about your lips, tongue and jaw positions for the target sound.*

1. _____ 3. _____

2. _____ 4. _____

Lesson 26: Plosive consonants unvoiced [p] as in "put", voiced [b] as in "but"

Plosive consonants: The air passage is completely blocked by two speech organs, pressure is built up, and on sudden release an explosive sound or "plosion" is heard.

Speech organs position:
The lips are pressed tightly together and suddenly move to allow the compressed air to escape in a small explosion. This is [p] sound. Add voice for [b] sound.

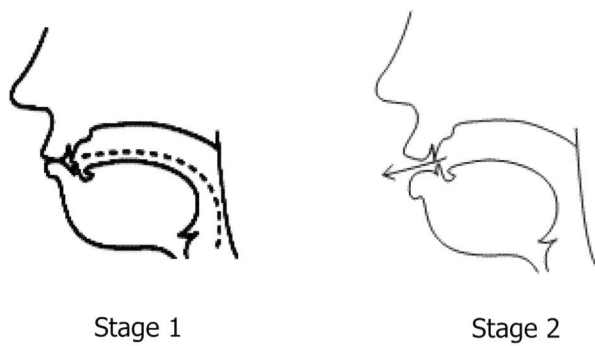

Stage 1   Stage 2

B10
🎧 **Repeat once from left to right:**

p	p	p	p
pp	pp	pp	p
ppp	ppp	ppp	p
pppp	pppp	pppp	p

B11
🎧 Words for unvoiced [p] sound

Listen and repeat. Look at the mouth diagram to help you position your lips, tongue and jaw for the target sound.

> **p**late, **p**lace, **p**antry, **p**arsley, **p**erform, **p**ublic, **p**resent, **p**rint, im**p**romptu, **p**leasant, **p**lace, **p**ersonal, **p**roperty, **p**reci**p**itate

B12
🎧 Sentences

Listen and repeat. Read each sentence aloud slowly at first, then as if you were telling it to someone in a natural way.

1. The **p**act on "**P**rivacy of **P**ersonal **P**roperty" was **p**rinted in the **p**aper.
2. He gave a **p**oor ex**p**lanation of the **p**ossibility of **p**ost**p**oning the **p**reliminary **p**lans to **p**ut a new **p**roduction manager in **p**lace.
3. **P**aul's **p**reposterous im**p**romptu **p**erformance was **p**retty **p**ersonal and lacked **p**ro**p**riety.
4. **P**enelo**p**e **p**romoted a healthy **p**easant a**pp**earance in her new s**p**ring com**p**ilation.
5. Although **p**izzas are **p**o**p**ular, most **p**eo**p**le **p**refer **p**retzels.
6. **P**ease **p**orridge hot, **p**ease **p**orridge cold, **p**ease **p**orridge in the **p**ot nine days old.

B13
🎧 Tongue-twister

Listen and copy the intonation and voice modulation on the CD.

Peter **P**i**p**er **p**icked a **p**eck of **p**ickled **p**e**pp**ers
A **p**eck of **p**ickled **p**e**pp**ers **P**eter **P**i**p**er **p**icked
If **P**eter **P**i**p**er **p**icked a **p**eck of **p**ickled **p**e**pp**ers
Where's the **p**eck of **p**ickled **p**e**pp**ers **P**eter **P**i**p**er **p**icked?

B14
🎧 Articulation exercise

Listen and repeat, keeping consonants clear and crisp.

A complicated gentleman allow me to present,
Of all the arts and faculties a terse embodiment:
A great arithmetician, who can demonstrate with ease,
That two and two are three or five, or anything you please:
An eminent logician, who can make it clear to you
That black is white — when looked at from the proper point of view:
A marvellous philologist, who'll undertake to show,
That "yes" is but another form of "no".
(*W.S. Gilbert*)

B15
🎧 Repeat once from left to right:

b	b	b	b
bb	bb	bb	b
bbb	bbb	bbb	b
bbbb	bbbb	bbbb	b

B16
🎧 Words for voiced [b]

Listen and repeat. Look at the mouth diagram to help you position your lips, tongue and jaw for the target sound.

b	bring, **b**aby, **B**ob, sno**b**, **b**omb, **b**alm
Nasal plosion	ca**b**man, su**b**mit, su**b**marine, so**b** noisily
Labial and lateral plosion	**b**a**bb**le, trou**b**le, go**bb**le, ta**b**le, dou**b**le

B17
🎧 Sentences

Listen and repeat. Read each sentence aloud slowly at first, then as if you were telling it to someone in a natural way.

1. **B**ill **B**o**bb**y **b**ought a **b**ig **b**lack ca**b** and **b**ecame a trou**b**led ca**b**man.
2. The **B**i**b**le on the ta**b**le **b**elonged to **B**renda **B**lenkin.
3. It was **b**rilliant **b**ursting **b**u**bb**les in their **b**illions during the **b**all in **B**elgravia.
4. **B**o**bb**y and **B**renda saw a **b**lack **b**at and a **b**ig **b**umble **b**ee at a **b**ar**b**ecue with their neigh**b**ours.
5. The **b**lack**b**ird **b**uilt a **b**eautiful **b**ig nest.

B18
🎧 Comparison: [p] and [b]

[p]	[b]
pocket	**b**ucket
piece	**b**ees
pork	**b**ark
point	**b**oiled
panther	**b**ender
passport	**b**uzzword

B19
🎧 Tongue-twister: the voiced [b] sound

Instructions: Copy the intonation and modulate the voice after the CD.

Betty **B**otter **b**ought some **b**utter,
But, she said the **b**utter's **b**itter;
If I put it in my **b**atter
It will make my **b**atter **b**itter,
But a **b**it of **b**etter **b**utter,
That would make my **b**atter **b**etter.

B20
🎧 Articulation exercise

Instructions: Make consonants clear and crisp.

Bibby Bobby bought a bat; Bibby Bobby bought a ball,
With that bat he banged the ball, banged it bump against the wall,
But so boldly Bobby banged, soon he burst the rubber ball.
Boo sobbed Bobby, goodbye ball. Bad luck, Bobby, bad luck ball.
Now to drown his many troubles, Bibby Bobby's blowing bubbles!

Additional exercises:

A: *Write down 4 words with the target sound that you often use when speaking English. Practice these words, thinking about your lips, tongue and jaw positions for the target sound.*

1. _____ 3. _____

2. _____ 4. _____

B: *Write down 4 words with the target sound that you often hear on TV, radio or from your friends/colleagues. Practice these words, thinking about your lips, tongue and jaw positions for the target sound.*

1. _____ 3. _____

2. _____ 4. _____

Lesson 27: Plosive consonants unvoiced [t] as in "two", voiced [d] as in "do"

Speech organs position:

The tip of the tongue contacts the alveolar ridge and suddenly moves down to allow the compressed air to escape in a small explosion. This is [t] sound. Add voice for [d] sound.

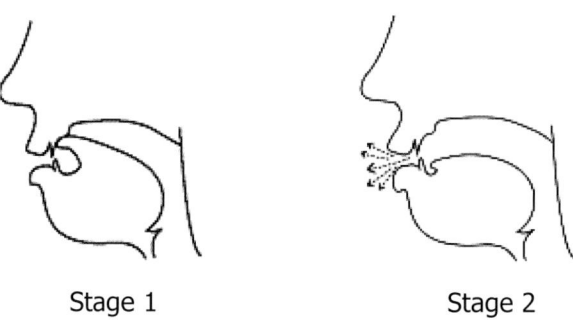

Stage 1   Stage 2

B21

🎧 **Repeat once from left to right:**

t	t	t	t
tt	tt	tt	t
ttt	ttt	ttt	t
tttt	tttt	tttt	t

B22

🎧 **Words: unvoiced [t] sound**

Listen and repeat. Look at the mouth diagram to help you position your lips, tongue and jaw for the target sound.

ten, tiny, tortoise, taught, try, test, text, flute, tutor, tots, turn, table, tennis, trot, tumultuous, tactless, terrific, traffic, totalitarian

B23

🎧 Sentences: unvoiced [t] sound

Listen and repeat. Read each sentence aloud slowly at first, then as if you were telling it to someone in a natural way.

1. Students taught by a private tutor from Eton passed all university tests with outstanding results.
2. Little tots were shocked by the tumultuous shouting sound of the waters.
3. When playing table tennis, take turns every thirty minutes to avoid fatigue.
4. Try to teach tots with tolerance and tact.
5. The river Trent tends to be a trickle rather than a torrent.

B24

🎧 Verses

Listen and copy the intonation and voice modulation on the CD.

Timothy Titus took two ties
To tie two tulips to two tall trees,
To terrify the terrible Thomas and
Tullamees.

B25

🎧 Repeat once from left to right:

d	d	d	d
dd	dd	dd	d
ddd	ddd	ddd	d
dddd	dddd	dddd	d

B26
🎧 **Words: voiced [d] sound**

Listen and repeat. Look at the mouth diagram to help you position your lips, tongue and jaw for the target sound.

diligent, **d**rought, **d**urable, **d**id, **d**one, **d**rill, **d**rag, **d**well, **d**angerous, **d**amage, **d**iminish, **d**iversifie**d**, **d**andruff, **d**owndraft, **d**edicate

B27
🎧 **Comparison: [t] and [d]**

[t]	[d]
car**t**	car**d**
tell	**d**well
wri**t**e	ri**d**e
tree	**d**ream
trout	**d**rought
tart	bar**d**

B28
🎧 **Sentences: voiced [d] sound**

Listen and repeat. Read each sentence aloud slowly at first, then as if you were telling it to someone in a natural way.

1. **D**unhill's **d**ue **d**iligence reveale**d** **d**ouble stan**d**ar**d**s in the pro**d**uction of **d**ifferent bran**d**s.
2. **D**ouglas' **d**aughter **D**eborah turne**d** out to be a **d**istinguished **d**ancer.
3. I've studie**d** the **d**ocumentation for the new ki**d**ney **d**rug in **d**etail.
4. The **d**edicate**d** student **d**evoted to **d**rama achieve**d** **d**ramatic results of immense **d**epth.
5. **D**uke **D**ouglas **d**ealt mainly with **d**ucks and **d**rakes.

76

B29
𝕲 Verses

Listen and copy the intonation and voice modulation on the CD.

Tormente**d** with the
anguish **d**rea**d**
Of falsehoo**d** unatone**d**,
I lay upon my sleepless
be**d**,
An**d** tossed an**d** turne**d**
an**d** groane**d**.

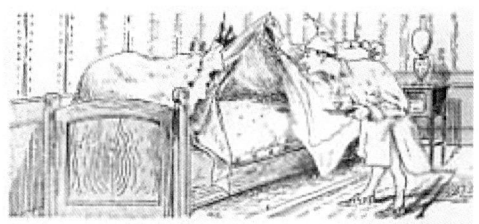

B30
𝕲 Articulation exercise

Listen and repeat, keeping consonants clear and crisp.

What a to do to die today at a minute or two to two
A thing distinctly hard to say but harder still to do
For they'll beat a tattoo at twenty to two a Ra ta ta ta ta ta ta ta ta too
And the dragon will come when he hears the drum
At a minute or two to two today at a minute or two to two.

Additional exercises:

A: *Write down 4 words with the target sound that you often use when speaking English. Practice these words, thinking about your lips, tongue and jaw positions for the target sound.*

1. _____ 3. _____

2. _____ 4. _____

B: *Write down 4 words with the target sound that you often hear on TV, radio or from your friends/colleagues. Practice these words, thinking about your lips, tongue and jaw positions for the target sound.*

1. _____ 3. _____

2. _____ 4. _____

Lesson 28: Plosive consonants unvoiced [k] as in "cake", voiced [g] as in "go"

Speech organs position:

The back of the tongue contacts the soft palate at the back of the mouth and suddenly moves down to allow the compressed air to escape in a small explosion. This is [k] sound. Add voice for [g] sound.

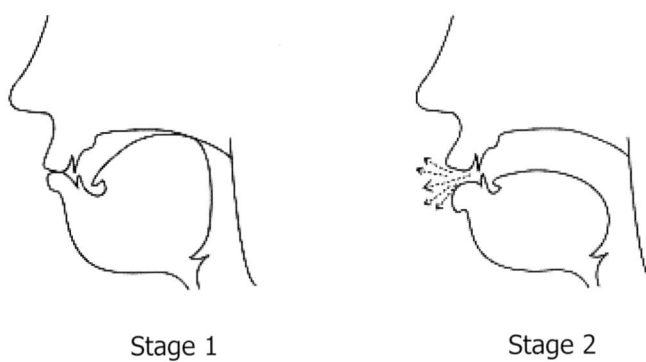

Stage 1   Stage 2

B31
🎧 Repeat once from left to right:

k	k	k	k
kk	kk	kk	k
kkk	kkk	kkk	k
kkkk	kkkk	kkkk	k

B32
🎧 Words: the unvoiced [k] sound

Listen and repeat. Look at the mouth diagram to help you position your lips, tongue and jaw for the target sound.

Spelling variations for the [k] sound	Highlighted bold letters pronounced as [k]
k	s**k**etch, **k**eep, **K**enya, **k**etchup, **k**ey, **k**ind
q	**q**uite, **q**uick, re**q**uest, s**q**ueeze, anti**q**ue
c	**c**at, **c**urious, magi**c**, un**c**le, histori**c**al, holisti**c**
ch	**ch**arismatic, stoma**ch**, **ch**emist, **ch**aos, **ch**ord

78

B33

🎧 Sentences: the unvoiced [k] sound

Listen and repeat. Read each sentence aloud slowly at first, then as if you were telling it to someone in a natural way.

1. **K**urt **c**an't **k**eep his **c**ool when **c**riticised by his un**c**le.
2. **C**atastrophi**c** reper**c**ussions **c**oncerning **ch**aotic **c**onfusion in **c**leri**c**al **c**ir**c**les were **k**ept **q**uiet.
3. For a sna**ck C**liff had **c**runchy **c**risps, **c**ake with **c**reamy **c**ustard and a **c**up of mil**k**y **c**offee.
4. **Ch**arismatic **C**lara was **k**een to wear **k**inky **c**lothes.
5. **C**onstance **c**olle**c**ted **c**oins and **c**ostumes from **C**anada and **C**ambodia.

B34

🎧 Verses

Listen and copy the intonation and voice modulation on the CD.

There was a **c**roo**k**ed man,
And he wal**k**ed a **c**roo**k**ed mile,
He found a **c**roo**k**ed sixpence
Against a **c**roo**k**ed stile;
He bought a **c**roo**k**ed **c**at,
Which **c**aught a **c**roo**k**ed mouse,
And they all lived together
In a little **c**roo**k**ed house.

B35
🎧 Repeat once from left to right:

g	g	g	g
gg	gg	gg	g
ggg	ggg	ggg	g
gggg	gggg	gggg	g

B36
🎧 Words: voiced [g] sound

Listen and repeat. Look at the mouth diagram to help you position your lips, tongue and jaw for the target sound.

Spelling variations for the [g] sound	Highlighted bold letters pronounced as [g]
g	**g**uessed, **g**uard, **g**host, pla**g**ue, **g**lue, strug**g**le, an**g**le, sin**g**le, si**g**nal, lan**g**uage
x-[gz]	e**x**act, e**x**amination, e**x**aggerate, e**x**ert, e**x**asperate, e**x**isting

B37
🎧 Comparison: [k] and [g]

[k]	[g]
creasy	graze
request	rugby
climax	glass
coast	ghost
con	gone

B38
🎧 Sentences: voiced [g] sound

Listen and repeat. Read each sentence aloud slowly at first, then as if you were telling it to someone in a natural way.

1. **G**ladys **g**lanced at **G**raham and **g**ave him a va**g**ue **g**ig**g**le.
2. **G**race strug**g**led with her **G**reek **g**rammar e**x**am and was **g**lad to **g**et a **g**reat **g**rade.
3. **G**ilbert **G**reen is no lon**g**er a sin**g**le **g**uy.
4. **G**racious **G**loria **g**azed at the e**x**aggerated **g**leaming **g**lobe.

5. "**G**ood **g**racious," the **g**rey **gh**ost said, "the fo**g** is **g**etting thicker."

B39
🎧 Tongue-twister

Listen and copy the intonation and voice modulation on the CD.

Three **g**rey **g**eese in a **g**reen field **g**razing,
Green were the **g**eese and **g**reen was the **g**razing.

B40
🎧 Articulation exercise

Listen and repeat, keeping consonants clear and crisp.

pt	**pt**	**pt**	**pt**
kt	**kt**	**kt**	**kt**
ptkt	**ptkt**	**ptkt**	**ptkt**
bd	**bd**	**bd**	**bd**
gd	**gd**	**gd**	**gd**
bdgd	**bdgd**	**bdgd**	**bdgd**

Additional exercises:

A: *Write down 4 words with the target sound that you often use when speaking English. Practice these words, thinking about your lips, tongue and jaw positions for the target sound.*

1. _____   3. _____

2. _____   4. _____

B: *Write down 4 words with the target sound that you often hear on TV, radio or from your friends/colleagues. Practice these words, thinking about your lips, tongue and jaw positions for the target sound.*

1. _____   3. _____

2. _____   4. _____

Lesson 29: Nasal consonant [m] as in "money"

Nasal consonants: A sound formed by a complete closure in the mouth by speech organs. The soft palate is lowered so that the air is free to pass out through the nose.

Speech organs position:
The lips come together
so that the breath cannot
be released through the
mouth. It escapes through
the nose where the sound
is produced.

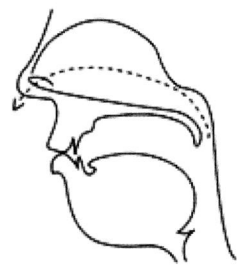

B41
🎧 Words: the [m] sound

Listen and repeat. Look at the mouth diagram to help you position your lips, tongue and jaw for the target sound.

> **m**ove, i**mm**ortal, co**m**b, s**m**oke, asth**m**a, pris**m**, **m**elody, **m**averick, **m**elancholic, **M**anchester, **m**irror, **m**onster, **m**i**m**osa, **m**eaning

B42
🎧 Sentences: the [m] sound

Listen and repeat. Read each sentence aloud slowly at first, then as if you were telling it to someone in a natural way.

1. The **m**anager fro**m** **M**anchester reco**mm**ended **m**aking **m**ore **m**oney.
2. **M**ozart's **m**elancholic **m**elodies have botto**m**less **m**eaning.
3. "The **m**oon looks like a **m**ottled **m**elon," **m**ur**m**ured **M**ark.
4. **M**argaret **m**ust be on ti**m**e for her **m**orning lessons in **m**i**m**e.
5. **M**obiles **m**ade in **M**alaysia **m**eet the needs of the **m**ost de**m**anding of custo**m**ers.
6. **M**innie **M**ouse was **m**oving to the chas**m** in the **m**arble **m**ausoleum.

B43

🎧 Tongue-twister: the [m] sound

Listen and copy the intonation and voice modulation on the CD.

Hie to the **m**arket, **Mim**i co**m**e trot,
Spilt all her butter **m**ilk, every drop.
Every drop and every dra**m**,
Mimi ca**m**e ho**m**e with an e**m**pty can.

B44

🎧 Articulation exercise

Listen and repeat, keeping consonants clear and crisp.

My boy you may take it from me,
That of all the afflictions accursed
With which a man's saddled and hampered and addled,
A diffident nature's the worst.
Though clever as clever can be
A Crichton of early romance
You must stir it and stump it and blow your own trumpet,
Or trust me you haven't a chance!

Now take for example my case
I've a bright intellectual brain
In all London city there's no one so witty –
I thought so again and again.
I've a highly intelligent face –
My features cannot be denied –
But whatever I try, Sir, I fail in, and why Sir?
I'm modesty personified!
(*W.S. Gilbert*)

Lesson 30: Nasal consonant [n] as in "no"

Speech organs position:
The tip of the tongue is on the alveolar ridge so that the breath cannot be released through the mouth. It escapes through the nose where the sound is produced.

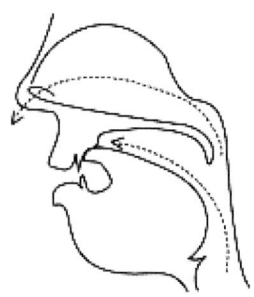

B45
🎧 Words

Listen and repeat. Look at the mouth diagram to help you position your lips, tongue and jaw for the target sound.

Spelling variations for the [n] sound	Highlighted bold letters pronounced as [n]
n	**n**oble, **n**un**n**ery, **n**imble, **n**aughty, **n**ine, **n**ever, **n**est, law**n**, daw**n**, upo**n**, dow**n**, pe**n**ny, agai**n**, so**n**
kn	**kn**ickers, **kn**it, **kn**owledge, **kn**own

B46
🎧 Sentences

Listen and repeat. Read each sentence aloud slowly at first, then as if you were telling it to someone in a natural way.

1. **N**ina wouldn't give her phone **n**umber to just a**n**yone.
2. I **n**either understand **n**or instantly admire ig**n**orant, **n**arrow-minded, opi**n**io**n**ated men without i**n**ner fire.
3. A**nn**e finds the **n**ews from foreig**n** countries i**n**formative a**n**d i**n**teresting.
4. **N**aughty **N**ick sneaked off to Aunt A**nn**ie's bar**n** and **n**apped till **n**oon like a baboo**n**.
5. At **n**ine in the morning, the train for **N**ottingham comes dow**n** the line.
6. **N**either **N**ina **n**or **N**ita **n**eeded **n**ew **kn**itted **kn**ickers.

84

B47
🎧 Verses

Listen and copy the intonation and voice modulation on the CD.

For every evil u**n**der the su**n**,
There is a remedy or there is **n**o**n**e.
If there be o**n**e, try a**n**d fi**n**d it;
If there be **n**o**n**e, **n**ever mi**n**d it.

Additional exercises:

A: *Write down 4 words with the target sound that you often use when speaking English. Practice these words, thinking about your lips, tongue and jaw positions for the target sound.*

1. _____ 3. _____

2. _____ 4. _____

B: *Write down 4 words with the target sound that you often hear on TV, radio or from your friends/colleagues. Practice these words, thinking about your lips, tongue and jaw positions for the target sound.*

1. _____ 3. _____

2. _____ 4. _____

Lesson 31: Nasal consonant [ŋ] as in "sing"

Speech organs position:
The tip of the tongue is
behind the bottom teeth,
and the back of the tongue
rises to contact the soft
palate, so the breath cannot
be released through the mouth.
It escapes through the nose,
where the sound is produced.

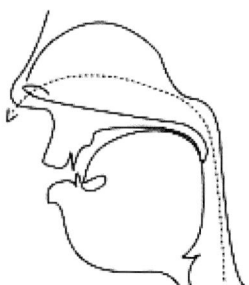

B48
🎧 Words: the [ŋ] sound

Listen and repeat. Look at the mouth diagram to help you position your lips, tongue and jaw for the target sound.

Spelling variations for [ŋ]	Highlighted bold letters pronounced as [ŋ]
ng	wi**ng**, si**ng**, su**ng**, ri**ng**, ha**ng**, bri**ng**, cli**ng**, sti**ng**, amo**ng**, to**ng**ue, nothi**ng**, saili**ng**, raili**ng**
n before k	thi**n**k, wi**n**k, ba**n**k, ho**n**k

B49
🎧 Sentences: the [ŋ] sound

Listen and repeat. Read each sentence aloud slowly at first, then as if you were telling it to someone in a natural way.

1. The you**ng** si**ng**er was si**ng**i**ng** a rousi**ng** so**ng**.
2. At the begi**nn**i**ng** of this mor**n**i**ng**'s class we were practici**ng** to**ng**ue exercises.
3. Without thi**nk**i**ng**, the Ki**ng** swu**ng** on the bell and it ra**ng** with a ti**ng**-a-li**ng**.
4. Payi**ng** rent, commuti**ng**, eati**ng** and dri**nk**i**ng** has been taki**ng** all the money I was ear**n**i**ng** from typi**ng**, writi**ng** and publicisi**ng**.
5. Supposi**ng** he is comi**ng** for a meeti**ng**, will you be telli**ng** him about separati**ng** and leavi**ng** Hasti**ng**s?

B50
🎧 Verses: the [ŋ] sound

Listen and copy the intonation and voice modulation on the CD.

Gaily tripp**ing**,
Lightly skipp**ing**,
Flock the maidens to the shipp**ing**.
Flags and guns and pennants
dipp**ing**!
All the ladies love the shipp**ing**.
(*W.S. Gilbert*)

Additional exercises:

A: *Write down 4 words with the target sound that you often use when speaking English. Practice these words, thinking about your lips, tongue and jaw positions for the target sound.*

1. _____ 3. _____

2. _____ 4. _____

B: *Write down 4 words with the target sound that you often hear on TV, radio or from your friends/colleagues. Practice these words, thinking about your lips, tongue and jaw positions for the target sound.*

1. _____ 3. _____

2. _____ 4. _____

Lesson 32: Nasal plosions [tn₁] as in "cotton", [dn₁] as in "garden"

Speech organs position:
When the nasal consonant [n] is preceded by either of the plosive consonants [t] or [d], the tip of the tongue stays on the alveolar ridge, while the two sounds are made at the same time and the breath escapes through the nose.

B51
🎧 Words

Listen and repeat. Look at the mouth diagram to help you position your lips, tongue and jaw for the target sound.

tn₁   mutton, cotton, button, eaten, Eton, threaten, kitten, curtain, certain, heighten, tighten, fatten, frighten, beaten

dn₁   hidden, burden, sadden, Haydn, pardon, sudden, madden, maiden, gladden, harden, suddenly, garden, modern

B52
🎧 Sentences

Listen and repeat. Read each sentence aloud slowly at first, then as if you were telling it to someone in a natural way.

[tn₁]
1. For my graduation from **Eton**, I cer**tain**ly need a nice white cot**ton** shirt with but**ton**s.
2. The police threa**ten**ed to tigh**ten** the rules for entering the country.
3. You must always be cer**tain** to tigh**ten** the cords when hanging your cur**tain**s.

[dn₁]
1. I would be glad to get rid of some bur**den**s of our mo**dern** life.
2. A frightened mai**den** has been hid**den** in the rear gar**den**.
3. Hay**dn** is not a mo**dern** composer but his music will either sad**den**, glad**den** or mad**den** you.

B53
🎧 Verses

Listen and copy the intonation and voice modulation on the CD.

Three little kit**ten**s
They lost their mit**ten**s,
And they began to cry:
Oh, mother dear,
We sadly fear
Our mit**ten**s we have lost.
What! Lost your mit**ten**s,
You naughty kit**ten**s!
Then you shall have no pie.

B54
🎧 Articulation exercise

Listen and repeat, keeping consonants clear and crisp.

Major-General

I am the very model of a modern Major-General
I've information vegetable, animal and mineral.
I know the kings of England and I quote the
fights historical
From Marathon to Waterloo, in order
categorical;
I'm very well acquainted too with matters
mathematical.
I understand equations, both the simple and
quadratical,
About binomial theorem I'm teeming with a lot
of news –
With many cheerful facts about the square of
the hypotenuse.
I'm very good at integral and differential calculus;
I know the scientific names of beings animalculous;
In short, in matters vegetable, animal and mineral,
I am the very model of a modern Major-General.
(*W.S. Gilbert*)

Lesson 33: Lateral consonant [l] as in "light"

Speech organs position:
The tip of the tongue is
on the alveolar ridge and
the back of the tongue is down.
The breath escapes from
the sides of the tongue.
The sound is voiced.

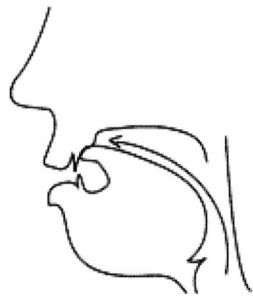

B55
🎧 Words

Listen and repeat. Look at the mouth diagram to help you position your lips, tongue and jaw for the target sound.

> leave, last, letter, love, lend, alone, allow, silly, chilly, fellow, shallow, holy, hollow, believe, place, plastic, blame, blue, blood, glue, glow, click, cloth, clumsy, club

B56
🎧 Sentences

Listen and repeat. Read each sentence aloud slowly at first, then as if you were telling it to someone in a natural way.

1. Millions of letters, I believe, can be easily lost due to Royal Mail faults.
2. Luminous lamps light the whole hall marvellously.
3. Luke's ludicrous letters to Lucia are unbelievable.
4. She looked supple and elegant in her black Channel jacket.
5. Red leather, yellow leather, red leather, yellow leather.
6. Failure to calculate the yield of the field made the clever lad ill.

B57
🎧 Verses

Listen and copy the intonation and voice modulation on the CD.

The Nightingale told his tale
In his own melodious way!
The lowly vale
For the mountain vainly sighed,
To his humble wail
The echoing hills replied.

Additional exercises

A: *Write down 4 words with the target sound that you often use when speaking English. Practice these words, thinking about your lips, tongue and jaw positions for the target sound.*

1. _____ 3. _____

2. _____ 4. _____

B: *Write down 4 words with the target sound that you often hear on TV, radio or from your friends/colleagues. Practice these words, thinking about your lips, tongue and jaw positions for the target sound.*

1. _____ 3. _____

2. _____ 4. _____

Lesson 34: Lateral plosions [tlˌ] as in "little", [dlˌ] as in "candle"

Speech organs position:
When the lateral consonant [l] is preceded by either of the plosive consonants [t] or [d], the tip of the tongue stays on the alveolar ridge, while the two sounds are made at the same time and the breath escapes from the sides of the tongue.

B58
🎧 **Words**

Listen and repeat. Look at the mouth diagram to help you position your lips, tongue and jaw for the target sound.

tlˌ   cattle, subtle, settle, rattle, total, mental, gentle, kettle, battle, brittle, metal, mettle, capital, vital, gentlemen, little

dlˌ   riddle, saddle, cuddle, candle, noodle, meddle, medal, bundle, pedal, tidal, fiddle, handle, poodle, paddle, middle, bridal

B59
🎧 **Sentences**

Listen and repeat. Read each sentence aloud slowly at first, then as if you were telling it to someone in a natural way.

[tlˌ]
1. It is vital for a gentleman to be subtle.
2. Gentlemen, let's estimate the total capital gain from our Seattle metal factory sale.
3. Little Lilly is so silly to fall in love with little Billy.
4. The noise of the pistols in the battle caused the cattle to be unsettled.

[dlˌ]
1. Give a cuddle to that little poodle!
2. For our bridal candle-lit supper we enjoyed Thai noodles.
3. Paddling to the middle of the tidal river deserves a bundle of medals.

B60
🎧 Verses

Listen and copy the intonation and voice modulation on the CD.

Doctor Fri**dl**e went to Bri**ddl**e
In a shower of rain;
He stepped in a pu**ddl**e,
Right up to his mi**ddl**e,
And never went there again.

Of a li**ttl**e take a li**ttl**e,
You are kin**dl**y welcome too;
Of a li**ttl**e leave a li**ttl**e,
This matters so to do.

Additional exercises:

A: *Write down 4 words with the target sound that you often use when speaking English. Practice these words, thinking about your lips, tongue and jaw positions for the target sound.*

1. _____ 3. _____

2. _____ 4. _____

B: *Write down 4 words with the target sound that you often hear on TV, radio or from your friends/colleagues. Practice these words, thinking about your lips, tongue and jaw positions for the target sound.*

1. _____ 3. _____

2. _____ 4. _____

Lesson 35: Fricative consonants unvoiced [f] as in "fish", voiced [v] as in "very"

Fricative consonants: The air passage is narrowed so that the breath, in escaping, produces audible friction or a kind of hissing sound.

<u>Speech organs position:</u>
The top teeth gently make
contact with the bottom lip
and the air squeezes past.
This makes the [f] sound.
Add voice for [v] sound.

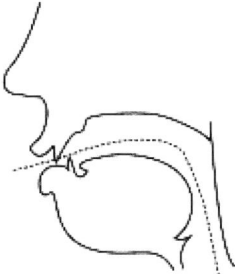

B61
🎧 Words: the unvoiced [f] sound

Listen and repeat. Look at the mouth diagram to help you position your lips, tongue and jaw for the target sound.

Spelling variations for the [f] sound	Highlighted bold letters pronounced as [f]
f	**f**east, **f**irst, cle**f**t, li**f**t, **f**antasy, **f**antastic, **f**inish
ft	so**ft**en, o**ft**en
ph	**ph**armacy, **ph**one, **ph**otogra**ph**, **ph**iloso**ph**y, **ph**ysics, **ph**ilharmonic
gh	rou**gh**, tou**gh**, lau**gh**

B62
🎧 Sentences: the unvoiced [f] sound

Listen and repeat. Read each sentence aloud slowly at first, then as if you were telling it to someone in a natural way.

1. **F**ormidable Ral**ph** was a true **ph**ilanthropist; in **f**act, he o**ft**en improved the li**f**e of those who **f**elt le**ft** out.
2. **Ph**ilip made an e**ff**ort to **f**ind his girl**f**riend's **f**avourite **f**uchsia **f**lowers.
3. An old **f**isherman lau**gh**ed when he caught **f**ive **f**resh **f**ish.
4. **F**rosty **f**rost in the **f**ridge was **f**reezing; we needed to **f**ix some **f**uel to de**f**rost the **f**ish **f**ingers.
5. The **f**i**ft**y **f**riends **f**rom **f**ar-**f**lung **f**oreign lands **f**ormed a **f**raternity.

94

B63
🎧 **Verses: the unvoiced [f] sound**

Listen and copy the intonation and voice modulation on the CD.

Freddy **f**armer went to **F**rinton
And went **f**ishing in the **f**og.
When he thought he'd caught a **f**ish
In **f**act he caught a **f**rog!

B64
🎧 **Words: the voiced [v] sound**

Listen and repeat. Look at the mouth diagram to help you position your lips, tongue and jaw for the target sound.

vote, **v**irtue, de**v**elop, re**v**i**v**e, **v**i**v**acious, in**v**olve, arri**v**e, con**v**ince, thri**v**e, sho**v**e, **v**acuum, Ste**v**en, re**v**i**v**al, **v**inegar, **v**olume, **v**elour

B65
🎧 **Comparison: [f] and [v]**

[f]	[v]
fat	**v**at
file	**v**ile
fail	**v**ale
shi**f**t	sho**v**e
e**ff**ort	e**v**idence
focus	**v**ocal

95

B66
🎧 Sentences: the voiced [v] sound

Listen and repeat. Read each sentence aloud slowly at first, then as if you were telling it to someone in a natural way.

1. Effervescent **V**era tried to achie**v**e mar**v**ellous results in **v**ain.
2. **V**indictive **v**endors con**v**inced naï**v**e **V**ictor to buy o**v**erpriced **v**elvet and **v**elour.
3. **V**ivacious **V**ivian lo**v**ed to **v**oice **v**igorous **v**erses **v**ociferously.
4. Ste**v**en **v**ainly **v**iewed **v**ast **v**ales with **v**acant eyes.
5. "There are **v**ery many **v**arieties of **v**egetation on our **v**eranda," said **V**era.

B67
🎧 Verses: the [v] sound

Listen and copy the intonation and voice modulation on the CD.

Vera **v**aulted **v**ainly o**v**er the garden wall,
Vera **v**ery nearly had a nasty fall.

Additional exercises:

A: *Write down 4 words with the target sound that you often use when speaking English. Practice these words, thinking about your lips, tongue and jaw positions for the target sound.*

1. _____ 3. _____

2. _____ 4. _____

B: *Write down 4 words with the target sound that you often hear on TV, radio or from your friends/colleagues. Practice these words, thinking about your lips, tongue and jaw positions for the target sound.*

1. _____ 3. _____

2. _____ 4. _____

Lesson 36: Unvoiced consonant [θ] as in "think"

Speech organs position:
The tip of the tongue comes between the top and bottom lip and the air squeezes past. This makes [θ] sound.

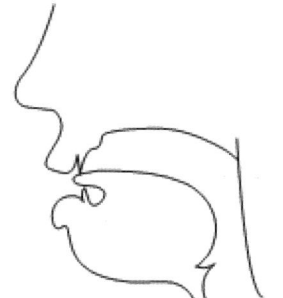

B68
🎧 **Words**

Listen and repeat. Look at the mouth diagram to help you position your lips, tongue and jaw for the target sound.

> **th**　　**th**anks, **th**ree, **th**ird, **th**ought, **th**umb, **th**ing, **th**in, ba**th**, brea**th**, clo**th**, ten**th**, six**th**, tru**th**, bo**th**, au**th**or, ari**th**metic

B69
🎧 **Sentences**

Listen and repeat. Read each sentence aloud slowly at first, then as if you were telling it to someone in a natural way.

1. **Th**ree fil**th**y looking **th**ieves were hiding in the **th**icket of **th**orny **th**istle bushes.
2. The au**th**or revealed the uncou**th** tru**th** in his latest **th**riller.
3. **Th**elma **th**ought that **th**eocratic **th**inking was **th**rilling.
4. Ari**th**metical **th**eorems come from **th**orough **th**inking of en**th**usiastic ari**th**meticians.
5. One weal**th**y au**th**or only wrote the tru**th** and not fil**th**.

B70
🎧 Comparison: [t] and [θ]

[t]	[θ]
taught	thought
trick	thick
tin	thin
note	north
matt	mouth
trade	thread
wet	hearth

B71
🎧 Tongue-twister

Listen and copy the intonation and voice modulation on the CD.

A **Th**atcher of **Th**atchwood went to
Thatcher a-**th**atching;
Did the of **Th**atcher of **Th**atchwood
go to **Th**atcher a-**th**atching?
If a **Th**atcher of **Th**atchwood went
to **Th**atcher a-**th**atching,
Where is the **th**atching **th**e
thatcher of **Th**atchwood has
thatched?

Additional exercises:

A: *Write down 4 words with the target sound that you often use when speaking English. Practice these words, thinking about your lips, tongue and jaw positions for the target sound.*

1. _____ 3. _____

2. _____ 4. _____

B: *Write down 4 words with the target sound that you often hear on TV, radio or from your friends/colleagues. Practice these words, thinking about your lips, tongue and jaw positions for the target sound.*

1. _____ 3. _____

2. _____ 4. _____

Lesson 37: Voiced consonant [ð] as in "that"

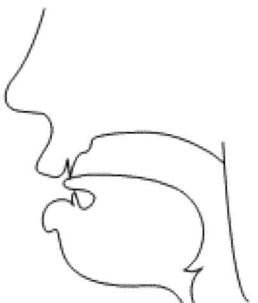

Speech organs position:

The tip of the tongue comes between the top lip and bottom lip and the air squeezes past. Add voice for [ð] sound.

B72

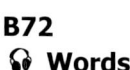 **Words**

Listen and repeat. Look at the mouth diagram to help you position your lips, tongue and jaw for the target sound.

> though, that, therefore, than, bathe, with, smooth, clothe, soothe, breathe, father, other, gather, rather, further, either

B73

🎧 **Sentences**

Listen and repeat. Read each sentence aloud slowly at first, then as if you were telling it to someone in a natural way.

1. This medicine is soothing for my rather sore back.
2. I would rather buy this leather hat than that one with the feathers.
3. My mother and father adore my younger brother for being rather smarter than I.
4. That brown leather coat is made of smoother leather than that black one in the window.
5. The southerly wind blew this way and that across the Scottish heather.

B74
🎧 **Verses**

Listen and copy the intonation and voice modulation on the CD.

The soldiers of our Queen
Are linked in friendly te**th**er;
Upon **th**e battle scene
They fight **th**e foe toge**th**er.
There every mo**th**er's son
Prepared to fight and fall is;
The enemy of one
The enemy of all is!
(*W.S. Gilbert*)

Additional exercises:

A: *Write down 4 words with the target sound that you often use when speaking English. Practice these words, thinking about your lips, tongue and jaw positions for the target sound.*

1. _____ 3. _____

2. _____ 4. _____

B: *Write down 4 words with the target sound that you often hear on TV, radio or from your friends/colleagues. Practice these words, thinking about your lips, tongue and jaw positions for the target sound.*

1. _____ 3. _____

2. _____ 4. _____

Lesson 38: Unvoiced [s] as in "sip", voiced [z] as in "zoo"

Speech organs position:

The air travels along a narrow passage in the centre of the tongue and squeezes between the tip of the tongue and the alveolar ridge. This makes [s] sound. Add voice for [z] sound.

B75
🎧 Words: the unvoiced [s] sound

Listen and repeat. Look at the mouth diagram to help you position your lips, tongue and jaw for the target sound.

Spelling variations for the [s] sound	Highlighted bold letters pronounced as [s]
s	swan, base, chase, paradise, practise, promise, gas, atlas, takes
sc	scientific, science, scent
c	finance, cemetery, circumstances, receive

B76
🎧 Sentences: the unvoiced [s] sound

Listen and repeat. Read each sentence aloud slowly at first, then as if you were telling it to someone in a natural way.

1. Sort these books on the staircase as soon as you have a spare second.
2. For supper, we've been served tasty sword fish with lemon sauce and succulent salad.
3. The symphony seemed sad and sentimental.
4. Simon saw seven silver swifts in the sea.
5. Steven Smith stood seven foot six in his stocking feet.

B77
🎧 Verses: the unvoiced [s] sound

Listen and copy the intonation and voice modulation on the CD.

Steven thought he **s**ang **s**o **s**weetly
In his offi**c**e every day,
But **s**o tunele**ss** was his **s**inging
He was paid to go away...

B78
🎧 Words: the voiced [z] sound

Listen and repeat. Look at the mouth diagram to help you position your lips, tongue and jaw for the target sound.

Spelling variations for the [z] sound	Highlighted bold letters pronounced as [z]
z	**z**oom, **z**ealous, **z**ip, **z**ig**z**ag, **z**oo, **Z**urich, **z**inc, **z**ebra, **z**ero, **z**est, **Z**imbabwe
s	sci**ss**or**s**, u**s**e, doe**s**, ha**s**, i**s**, a**s**, wa**s**, ea**s**y, bu**s**y, dog**s**, tree**s**, play**s**, clean**s**e

B79
🎧 Comparison: [s] and [z]

[s]	[z]
dock**s**	dog**s**
hat**s**	home**s**
hit**s**	hum**s**
cake**s**	keg**s**
nit**s**	nun**s**
bit**s**	bib**s**

Voiced and unvoiced endings for plurals and third person singulars

Rule: If the sound before the ending is unvoiced then the ending will be unvoiced too. If the sound before the ending is voiced then the ending will be voiced.

Unvoiced sounds (sounds made with breath only)	Voiced sounds (sounds made with vibrations of vocal cords)
1) Consonant Pairs: [s] soup [p] pick [t] tick [k] kick [tʃ] church [ʃ] shoe [f] fan [θ] think **Unvoiced endings examples:** Cats, puffs, dusts, pipes, sorts, kicks, laughs, truths, cloths, moths, etc.	**1) Consonant Pairs:** [z] hose [b] bubble [d] dog [g] giggle [dʒ] George [ʒ] rouge [v] van [ð] that **2) Voiced nasal and lateral consonants:** [l] lock, [m] meter, [n] nun, [ŋ] king **3) All vowels and diphthongs** **Voiced endings examples:** Dogs, badges, massages, clothes, miles, nuns, ages, sandwiches, etc.

Don't confuse: The root of the word with the ending. Although the sound before "s" is voiced, and according to the rule it should be pronounced with [z], because it's the root of the word and not plural ending or third person singular ending, it will be pronounced with [s]: gas, atlas, this, genius; defensive, conclusive; university, curiosity, verbosity; base, staircase, case, chase, crease, decrease, grease, geese, concise, paradise, practise, promise, tortoise, use (noun); else, dense, lapse, course etc.

B80
🎧 **Sentences: the voiced [z] sound**

Listen and repeat. Read each sentence aloud slowly at first, then as if you were telling it to someone in a natural way.

1. Wise Moses had most reasonable ideas.
2. Joseph supposes that his toeses are roses.
3. Zeta rode a zebra in Zimbabwe.
4. Ideas do not fall from the trees.
5. Zoë spends pounds and pounds on snazzy shoes and gowns.
6. The bee buzzes lazily on the pansies, daisies and roses.

B81
🎧 **Verses: the voiced [z] sound**

Listen and copy the intonation and voice modulation on the CD.

Scissors and string, scissors and string,
When a man's single he lives like a king.
Needles and pins, needles and pins,
When a man marries his trouble begins.

Additional exercises:

A: *Write down 4 words with the target sound that you often use when speaking English. Practice these words, thinking about your lips, tongue and jaw positions for the target sound.*

1. _____ 3. _____

2. _____ 4. _____

B: *Write down 4 words with the target sound that you often hear on TV, radio or from your friends/colleagues. Practice these words, thinking about your lips, tongue and jaw positions for the target sound.*

1. _____ 3. _____

2. _____ 4. _____

Lesson 39: Unvoiced [ʃ] as in "shall", voiced [ʒ] as in "measure"

Speech organs position:

The tongue tip is near the bottom of the mouth and the air escapes along a passage in the centre of the tongue with lips slightly rounded.

This makes [ʃ] sound. Add voice for [ʒ] sound.

B82
🎧 Words: the unvoiced [ʃ] sound

Listen and repeat. Look at the mouth diagram to help you position your lips, tongue and jaw for the target sound.

Spelling variations for the [ʃ] sound	Highlighted bold letters pronounced as [ʃ]
sh	**sh**eep, **sh**irt, pu**sh**, wi**sh**, fa**sh**ion, ca**sh**ier
ch	mousta**ch**e, **ch**ampagne
s, ss	pre**ss**ure, **s**e**ss**ion, Ru**ss**ia, **s**ure, **S**ean
Spelling variations for the [ʃə] sound	Highlighted bold letters pronounced as [ʃə]
cio, cia	spe**cia**l, deli**cio**us, mali**cio**us, suspi**cio**us
tio, cia	condi**tio**n, mo**tio**n, nutri**tio**us, Vene**tia**n

B83
🎧 Sentences: the unvoiced [ʃ] sound

Listen and repeat. Read each sentence aloud slowly at first, then as if you were telling it to someone in a natural way.

1. I wi**sh** I **sh**opped for **sh**irts with fa**sh**ionable **Sh**eila.
2. I am under the suspi**ci**on that Ru**ss**ians can be quite emo**ti**onal.
3. During our spe**cia**l se**ss**ion on nutri**ti**on we wi**sh**ed to be served deli**ci**ous di**sh**es and **ch**ampagne.
4. **S**ean's **sh**iny **sh**oes are made from **sh**ark skin.
5. Mali**cio**us men with mousta**ch**es pre**ss**urised us to leave the **sh**ip.
6. **Sh**immering and **sh**ining hair needs a condi**ti**oner and **sh**ampoo.

B84
🎧 Tongue-twister: the unvoiced [ʃ] sound

Listen and copy the intonation and voice modulation on the CD.

She sells sea**sh**ells by the sea-**sh**ore;
If **sh**e sells sea**sh**ells by the sea-**sh**ore,
Then I'm **s**ure **sh**e sells sea-**sh**ore **sh**ells.

B85
🎧 Words: the voiced [ʒ] sound

Listen and repeat. Look at the mouth diagram to help you position your lips, tongue and jaw for the target sound.

Spelling variations for the [ʒ] sound	Highlighted bold letters pronounced as [ʒ]
s before **ur**	mea**s**ure, plea**s**ure, ca**s**ual, enclo**s**ure
s before **io**	occa**s**ion, deci**s**ion, confu**s**ion, intru**s**ion, colli**s**ion
g	presti**g**e, gara**g**e, massa**g**e, bei**g**e, rou**g**e

B86
🎧 Comparison: [ʃ] and [ʒ]

[ʃ]	[ʒ]
condi**tio**n	colli**si**on
shoes	unu**su**al
a**ss**ure	ca**su**al
vi**ci**ous	vi**si**on
vaca**tio**ns	occa**si**on
devo**tio**n	deci**si**on

B87

🎧 **Sentences: the voiced [ʒ] sound**

Listen and repeat. Read each sentence aloud slowly at first, then as if you were telling it to someone in a natural way.

1. Charles trea**su**red the prest**i**ge of his house and disliked sudden intru**si**on.
2. The plea**su**rable occa**si**on ended in a judicial colli**si**on due to faulty vi**si**on.
3. Disillu**si**oned **G**iselle felt confu**si**on regarding the disclo**su**re of the family trea**su**re.
4. Watching televi**si**on without mea**su**re can be a limiting plea**su**re.
5. The girl u**su**ally uses red rou**g**e but she decided to change to bei**g**e.

B88

🎧 **Verses: the voiced [ʒ] sound**

Listen and copy the intonation and voice modulation on the CD.

Oh, marvellous illu**si**on!
Or, terrible surprise!
What is this strange confu**si**on
That veils my aching eyes?

B89

🎧 **Articulation exercise**

Listen and repeat, keeping consonants clear and crisp.

In enterprise of martial kind,
When there was any fighting,
He led his regiment from behind –
He found it less exciting.
But when away his regiment run,
His place was at the fore, O –
That celebrated,
Cultivated,
Underrated nobleman,
The Duke of Plaza Toro!
(*W.S. Gilbert*)

Additional exercises:

A: *Write down 4 words with the target sounds that you often use when speaking English. Practice these words, thinking about your lips, tongue and jaw positions for the target sound.*

1. _____ 3. _____

2. _____ 4. _____

B: *Write down 4 words with the target sounds that you often hear on TV, radio or from your friends/colleagues. Practice these words, thinking about your lips, tongue and jaw positions for the target sound.*

1. _____ 3. _____

2. _____ 4. _____

Lesson 40: Unvoiced consonant [h] as in "hat"

Speech organs position:
The space between the vocal
chords is narrowed as
air squeezes past to make
[h] sound.

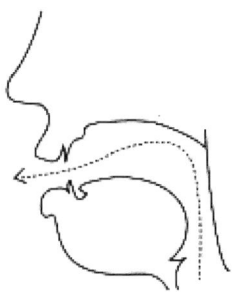

B90
🎧 Words

Listen and repeat. Look at the mouth diagram to help you position your lips, tongue and jaw for the target sound.

h	**h**at, **h**eat, **h**ard, **h**urt, **h**ideous, a**h**oy, be**h**ind, be**h**ave, per**h**aps, boy**h**ood, re**h**earse, en**h**ance, **h**eather, **h**eredity, in**h**erit, ad**h**ere, dis**h**earten, be**h**alf
wh	**wh**o

B91
🎧 Sentences

Listen and repeat. Read each sentence aloud slowly at first, then as if you were telling it to someone in a natural way.

1. On be**h**alf of the **wh**ole group, we say a **h**earty **h**ello.
2. Be**h**ind **h**is **h**ideous be**h**aviour, which was **h**urting us to the very **h**eart, was **h**is **h**ard child**h**ood.
3. In case of a **h**orrible **h**eadache, **h**eat **wh**olesome **h**eather **h**oney and in**h**ale it.
4. **H**eather in**h**erited **h**er father's **h**orrendously **h**uge **h**ouse in **H**ammersmith.
5. **H**ungarian **h**unters on **h**orses with **h**ounds were **h**orrified by **h**urricanes.
6. "**Wh**o," said **H**elen, "**h**as eaten **h**alf of my **h**oney cake?"

110

B92

🎧 Verses

Listen and copy the intonation and voice modulation on the CD.

Henry Harvey heaved a huge and heavy hammer,
A huge and heavy hammer Henry Harvey heaved,
If Henry Harvey heaved a huge and heavy hammer,
Where's the huge and heavy hammer Henry Harvey
heaved?

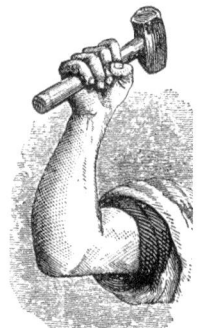

Additional exercises:

A: *Write down 4 words with the target sound that you often use when speaking English. Practice these words, thinking about your lips, tongue and jaw positions for the target sound.*

1. _____ 3. _____

2. _____ 4. _____

B: *Write down 4 words with the target sound that you often hear on TV, radio or from your friends/colleagues. Practice these words, thinking about your lips, tongue and jaw positions for the target sound.*

1. _____ 3. _____

2. _____ 4. _____

Lesson 41: The [r] sound as in "river"

Speech organs position:
The tip of the tongue curls back
slightly in the roof of the mouth,
just behind the alveolar ridge, and
the breath squeezes past.
This makes the [r] sound.

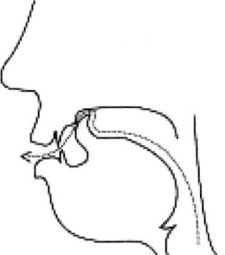

[r   r   r]

B93

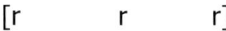 *Repeat once from left to right:*

[ru:	rəu	rɔ:	rɑ:	reɪ	ri:]
[pr u::	prəu	prɔ:	prɑ:	preɪ	pri:]
[spr u:	sprəu	sprɔ:	sprɑ:	spreɪ	spri:]
[gr u:	grəu	grɔ:	grɑ:	greɪ	gri:]
[br u:	brəu	brɔ:	brɑ:	breɪ	bri:]
[fr u:	frəu	frɔ:	frɑ:	freɪ	fri:]
[θr u:	θrəu	θrɔ:	θrɑ:	θreɪ	θri:]

B94
🎧 **Words**

*Listen and repeat. Look at the mouth diagram to help you position your lips, tongue and
jaw for the target sound.*

r	rang, rest, road, rock, rascal, rescue
pr	proof, proud, press, prank, pressure
spr	spread, sprawl, sprain, spring, sprout
cr	crime, crawl, cruise, cry, crept, cross
gr	grand, grain, grass, gravy, grows, grot
br	bring, brave, break, brute, browse
fr	fry, frame, fright, frank, frost, freeze
thr	thrift, threat, throb, through, thrill
rr	borrow, sorrow, carry, worry, carriage

B95
🎧 Sentences

Listen and repeat. Read each sentence aloud slowly at first, then as if you were telling it to someone in a natural way.

1. **R**ound and **r**ound the **r**ugged **r**ock, the **r**agged **r**ascal **r**an.
2. In spring, **R**ome is **r**eally very **pr**etty.
3. **R**ose **R**ochester's **r**ole emb**r**aces **pr**epa**r**ation of the **r**ole **pr**ofiles for **r**egional sales **r**eps.
4. I **r**ather **pr**efer **pr**awns on **r**ye b**r**ead to greasy po**r**k with g**r**avy and **r**ice.
5. **R**iding **r**ound the na**rr**ow **r**ace-track, **R**obert **r**an ove**r** a ho**rr**id b**r**own **r**at.

B96
🎧 Tongue-twister

Listen and copy the intonation and voice modulation on the CD.

Robert **R**owley **r**olled a **r**ound **r**oll **r**ound,
A **r**ound **r**oll **R**obert **R**owley **r**olled **r**ound;
Where **r**olled the **r**ound **r**oll
Robert **R**owley **r**olled **r**ound?

Additional exercises:

A: *Write down 4 words with the target sound that you often use when speaking English. Practice these words, thinking about your lips, tongue and jaw positions for the target sound.*

1. _____ 3. _____

2. _____ 4. _____

B: *Write down 4 words with the target sound that you often hear on TV, radio or from your friends/colleagues. Practice these words, thinking about your lips, tongue and jaw positions for the target sound.*

1. _____ 3. _____

2. _____ 4. _____

Lesson 42: Affricates unvoiced [tʃ] as in "church", voiced [dʒ] as in "judge"

Affricate consonants: The first part is a plosive consonant followed immediately by the second part, a fricative consonant.

Speech organs position:

Make the [t] "two" sound at the same time as making the [ʃ] "shall" sound. This makes the [tʃ] "church" sound.

Make the [d] "dog" sound at the same time as making the [ʒ] "measure" sound. This makes the [dʒ] "gin" sound.

B97
🎧 Words: the [tʃ] sound

Listen and repeat. Look at the mouth diagram to help you position your lips, tongue and jaw for the target sound.

Spelling variations for the [tʃ] sound	Highlighted bold letters pronounced as [tʃ]
ch	**ch**urch, **Ch**urchill, **ch**ap, whi**ch**, or**ch**ard, a**ch**ieve
tch	ca**tch**, bu**tch**er, clu**tch**ed, ma**tch**ed, Tha**tch**er
t before **u**	litera**tu**re, pos**tu**re, mois**tu**rise, architec**tu**re

B98
🎧 Sentences: the unvoiced [tʃ] sound

Listen and repeat. Read each sentence aloud slowly at first, then as if you were telling it to someone in a natural way.

1. The old **ch**ur**ch** in **Ch**ester represents the architec**tu**re of the eighteenth cen**tu**ry.
2. The lec**tu**re in **Ch**inese litera**tu**re was quite an adven**tu**re for the lec**tu**rer.
3. For lun**ch**, I had some **ch**ips with blue **ch**eese followed by **Ch**inese jasmine tea.
4. We **ch**eerfully **ch**ose **Ch**ippendale **ch**airs to ma**tch** our **ch**arming antique furni**tu**re.

114

5. They **ch**ased and sear**ch**ed for **Ch**arlie but they couldn't cat**ch** **h**im.

B99
🎧 Tongue-twister: the unvoiced [tʃ] sound

Listen and copy the intonation and voice modulation on the CD.

How mu**ch** wood would a wood**ch**uck **ch**uck
If a wood**ch**uck could **ch**uck wood?

B100
🎧 Words: the [dʒ] sound

Listen and repeat. Look at the mouth diagram to help you position your lips, tongue and jaw for the target sound.

Spelling variations for the [dʒ] sound	Highlighted bold letters pronounced as [dʒ]
j	**j**ob, ad**j**oin, **j**oke, **J**ohn, **J**une, **j**uvenile, re**j**ection
g	**g**em, lugga**g**e, ba**dg**er, le**dg**er, **G**eorge, coura**g**e

B101
🎧 Comparison: [tʃ] and [dʒ]

[tʃ]	[dʒ]
chur**ch**	ju**dg**e
chap	**g**y**p**
cheap	**g**in
chunk	**j**unk
choose	**j**uice
ba**tch**	bagga**g**e
adven**tu**re	avera**g**e

B102
🎧 Sentences: the voiced [dʒ] sound

Listen and repeat. Read each sentence aloud slowly at first, then as if you were telling it to someone in a natural way.

1. In **J**une and **J**uly the weather is **g**enerally en**j**oyable in this re**g**ion of **G**eor**g**ia.
2. **J**ohn was **j**ud**g**ing his wife for re**j**ections in his marria**g**e and his boss for in**j**ustice in his **j**ob.
3. These **g**herkins with **g**in**g**er and tomato **j**uice from the **j**ar are **j**olly good!
4. Even an avera**g**e **j**ud**g**e char**g**es too much!
5. The marria**g**e of **G**erald and **G**ina was ju**dg**ed to be **j**oyful.

B103
🎧 Verses: the voiced [dʒ] sound

Listen and copy the intonation and voice modulation on the CD.

Yes, now I'm a Ju**dg**e!
Though all my law be fu**dg**e,
Yet I'll never, never bu**dg**e,
But I'll live and die a Ju**dg**e!
And a good Ju**dg**e too!

B104
🎧 Articulation exercise

Listen and repeat, keeping consonants clear and crisp.

Oh a private buffoon is a light hearted loon,
If you listen to popular rumour.
From the morn to the night he's so joyous and bright
And he bubbles with wit and good humour.
He's so quaint and so terse, both in prose and in verse,
Yet though people forgive his transgressions,
There are one or two rules that all Family Fools
Must observe if they love their profession.
There are one or two rules, half a dozen maybe
That all Family Fools of whatever degree,
Must observe, if they love their profession.
(*W.S. Gilbert*)

116

The Speech Organs

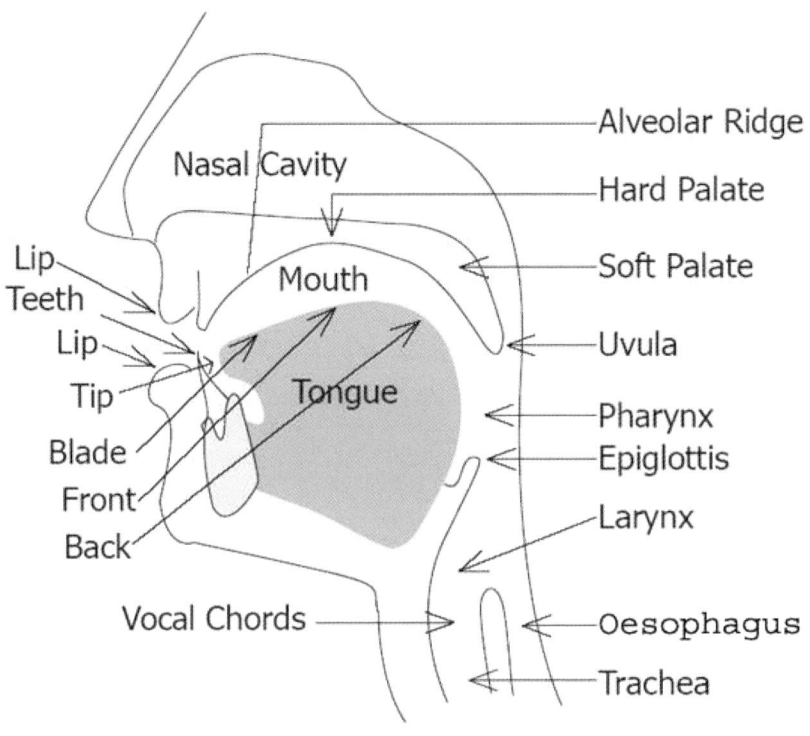

Alveolar Ridge

Nasal Cavity

Hard Palate

Lip
Teeth

Mouth

Soft Palate

Lip

Uvula

Tip

Tongue

Blade

Pharynx
Epiglottis

Front

Larynx

Back

Vocal Chords

Oesophagus

Trachea

Conclusion

Vowels
- Lean on long vowels and diphthongs; do not shorten them.
- Usually, words with long vowels sound prominent and reflect the rhythm of the language.
- Schwa is very short and unstressed. Very often vowels in unstressed position are pronounced as a schwa.
- Semi-vowels [j] and [w] are fully vocalised.

Consonants
- Make the consonants sound crisp and sharp before and after short vowels.
- Energetically enunciate fricatives [f-v, θ- ð, ʃ- ʒ, s-z, h] and plosives [t-d, p-b, k-g]; pronounce them with aspiration.
- Don't over-pronounce consonants, avoid pronouncing them harshly; in words with long vowels put emphasis on long vowels rather than over-articulating the consonant.

Sentence rhythm
- Do not separate words in a sentence; glide from one word to another like in a song.
- Stress the words which carry the most important meaning.
- Usually words with long vowels are stressed and sound prominent.
- Do not stress articles or prepositions; pronounce them with a schwa [ə].
- Often, unstressed vowels are pronounced with a schwa [ə].

Maintaining correct pronunciation

Now that you have practiced and trained your speech organs for English sounds, you've reached the stage where it's important to maintain correct pronunciation. Experience shows that it is easy to revert to your original foreign or regional accent if you do not continue making an effort to pronounce correctly.

Follow the advice in order to maintain correct pronunciation:

1. Avoid speaking in your native language. Speaking in your native language will prevent you from memorising the correct placement of the speech organs and developing the speech organ muscles for the English sounds.

2. Avoid speaking too fast, pronounce every syllable. Many people are not able to make clear sounds when speaking rapidly and these lead to indistinct or 'woolly' speech".

3. Do the warm-up exercise on page 121 for about 10 minutes every day.

4. Sounds which are particularly difficult for you to pronounce need to be practiced every day until you pronounce them correctly. See page 125.

5. Read newspapers, magazines and books out loud. Audio books are fantastic to listen to and to imitate the correct pronunciation.

6. Do regular weekly recording exercises:
   - Record yourself reading,
   - Listen to your tape,
   - Make a note of sounds where you made a mistake in pronunciation,
   - Practice the sounds where you made a mistake with this book.

7. Learn poems and read them expressively; modulate your voice.

8. Go to the theatre. Many actors will be using RP in their performances and provide a great example to follow.

9. Join public speaking clubs such as Toastmasters, literature societies and book clubs where you can continue to improve your speech. See www.earlybirdspeakers.co.uk for information.

Warm-up exercises

Tongue exercises

Instructions: All exercises to be repeated 4 times.

1. Point the tongue, holding it still. Then relax the tongue.
2. Point the tongue. Circle very slowly once to right. Repeat to left.
3. Point the tongue. Circle 3 times quickly to right. Then left.
4. Stretch the tongue towards the nose, then the chin.
5. With tip of tongue behind bottom teeth, push back of tongue forwards and backwards.
6. Flick pointed tongue sideways, touching corners of lips. Gradually quicken.
7. Tap tip of the tongue against alveolar (teeth) ridge. Repeat and quicken.
8. Finish off with rhythm exercises for [t], [d], [l], [k] and [g] sounds.

Example from page 74:
B21
🎧 Repeat once from left to right, keep the jaw relaxed and still:

t	t	t	t
tt	tt	tt	t
ttt	ttt	ttt	t
tttt	tttt	tttt	t

Lip exercises

Instructions: All exercises to be repeated 4 times.

1. With teeth closed, spread lips back to a broad smile, and then bring forward to a tight [uː] position as in "June".
2. Repeat exercise 1, but with jaw open about 1" (2.5 cm).
3. Make a chewing motion in all directions.
4. Keeping the bottom lip still, raise top lip towards nostrils. Bring lips together again. Quicken.
5. Keeping top lip still, move bottom lip down. Bring lips together again. Quicken.
6. Move top and bottom lips alternately. Quicken.
7. To relax the lips, blow through them very gently.
8. Finish off with rhythm exercises for [p], [b], [m] and [w] sounds. For example, exercise B10 on page 68, B15 on page 70 or B4 on page 64.

We have organised consonants according to the contact of two speech organs.

Instructions: Repeat each sentence 3 times.

C1
🎧 Two lips coming together

[m]
Matthew and **M**ichael were **m**asters of **m**ime and **m**ove**m**ent.

[p] unvoiced
Percival **P**ratt was **p**ermanently **p**laying **p**ing-**p**ong at **P**ortsmouth.

[b] voiced
The **b**race of **b**rown **b**irds was **b**agged **b**y **B**illy **B**utler.

[w]
I **w**ondered **w**hy you **w**andered a**w**ay **w**hen it **w**ould have been better to have **w**aited.

C2
🎧 Back of the tongue and soft palate

[k] unvoiced
Kenneth **K**ent was **c**ler**k** to the **c**ourt at **C**ambridge.

[g] voiced
Glorious **G**ainer **g**alloped **g**aily round the **g**ravel track.

[ŋ]
They sa**ng** a so**ng**, but the so**ng** they sa**ng** was wro**ng**.

C3
🎧 Tip of the tongue and alveolar ridge

[t] unvoiced
Timothy made **t**enta**t**ive at**t**empts at playing **t**ennis.

[d] voiced
Doubtless **D**ennis was **d**elighte**d** with his **d**ouble **d**amask **d**ressing gown.

[n] sound
Nearly every Su**n**day a**n**d Mo**n**day **n**ight, **N**adia sings **n**autical songs.

[l]
The **l**anky **L**ord of **L**ondon bui**l**t a cast**l**e and a mi**ll**.

[tlⱼ]
Fill the lit**tl**e me**tal** ket**tl**e from the bot**tl**e in the ante-na**tal** hospi**tal**.

[dlⱼ]
Don't fid**dl**e with the mid**dl**e bun**dl**e of can**dl**es.

[tnⱼ]
Mother threa**ten**ed to frigh**ten** the kit**ten** if it ate the mut**ton**.

[dnⱼ]
The mai**den** sud**den**ly discovered the hid**den** gar**den**.

[s] unvoiced
Simply **s**umptuou**s** **s**nack**s** **s**ati**s**fy **s**imple **s**ouls.

[z] voiced
Pri**z**e-winning a**z**alea**s** surpri**s**e a do**z**en do**z**y damsel**s**.

[r]
Th**r**ee **r**ed lo**rr**ies d**r**ove over the **r**usty **r**ailway b**r**idge.

C4
🎧 **Lower Lip and Upper Teeth**

[f] unvoiced
Ral**ph** was rou**gh** and tou**gh** but also **f**earless and **f**rank.
[v] voiced
Virtually e**v**eryone **v**oted to lea**v**e the **v**illage unde**v**eloped.

C5
🎧 **Tip of the tongue and Upper teeth**

[θ] unvoiced
Ma**th**ematical **th**eories and my**th**ical figures mix ma**ths** and my**ths**.

[ð] voiced
The boy wri**th**ed and see**th**ed wi**th** rage while being ba**th**ed by his loa**th**some mo**th**er.

C6
🎧 **Tip and blade of the tongue on alveolar ridge**

[tʃ] unvoiced
The **ch**urch warden **ch**ose the **ch**eap **ch**eese rather than the mu**ch** ri**ch**er lamb **ch**ops.

[dʒ] voiced
Geor**g**e had the coura**g**e to say that the porri**dg**e was avera**g**e.

C7
🎧 **Blade of the tongue on front palate**

[ʃ] unvoiced
Ma**ch**ine-made **sh**oes **sh**ould **s**urely be **sh**own in **sh**oe **sh**op windows.

[ʒ] voiced
After the colli**si**on I made a deci**si**on to drive to the gara**g**e and park with preci**si**on.

C8
🎧 **Breath and vocal chords**

[h]
In **H**ampstead, **H**astings and **H**ounslow, **h**amsters **h**ave been **h**arassed.

International Phonetic Alphabet

🎧 Long Pure Vowels

/iː/ - feet - /fiːt/
/ɜː/ – third – /θɜːd/
/uː/ – boot – /buːt/
/ɑː/ - bark – /bɑːk/
/ɔː/ – fort – /fɔːt/

🎧 Short Pure Vowels

/ɪ/ – pit – /pɪt/
/e/ – pet – /pet/
/æ/ – mad – /mæd/
/ʌ/ – hut – /hʌt/
/ɒ/ – box – /bɒks/
/ʊ/ – book – /bʊk/

Neutral Vowel (schwa)

/ə/ – the – /ðə/

🎧 Diphthongs

/ɪə/ – hear – /hɪə/
/eɪ/ – pay – /peɪ/
/eə/ – pair – /peə/
/aɪ/ – pie – /paɪ/
/aʊ/ – how – /haʊ/
/əʊ/ – boat – /bəʊt/
/ɔɪ/ – boy – /bɔɪ/
/ʊə/ – sewer – /sʊə/

🎧 Unvoiced Consonants

/p/ – put – /pʊt/
/t/ – two – /tuː/
/k/ – cake – /keɪk/
/f/ – fish – /fɪʃ/
/θ/ – think – /θɪŋk/
/s/ – sip – /sɪp/
/ʃ/ – shall – /ʃæl/
/tʃ/ – church – /tʃɜːtʃ/
/h/ – hat – /hæt/

🎧 Voiced Consonants

/b/ – but – /bʌt/
/d/ – do – /duː/
/g/ – go – /gəʊ/
/v/ – very – /veri/
/ð/ – that – /ðæt/
/z/ – zoo – /zuː/
/ʒ/ – measure – /meʒə/
/dʒ/ – judge – /dʒʌdʒ/

/m/ – money – /ˈmʌni/
/n/ – no – /nəʊ/
/ŋ/ – sing – /sɪŋ/
/l/ – light – /laɪt/
/r/ – river – /ˈrɪvə/
/j/ – yes – /jes/
/w/ – was – /wɒz/

Difficulties in pronunciation for speakers of world languages

As was outlined in the introduction, existence of an accent can be explained by the fact that some English sounds do not exist in your native language, and your speech organs are not trained for them. Therefore these sounds may represent a particular difficulty in pronunciation. Below we list speakers of world languages and their particular difficulties.

Main world language	Key countries where it is spoken	Particularly difficult English sounds	Recommendations
Arabic	Algeria, Egypt, Iraq, Jordan, Saudi Arabia, Syria, Tunisia, others	[r], [l], [tʃ], [ɔ:], [ɜ:]	Avoid aspirated trilled [r]
Chinese	China, Taiwan, Malaysia, Singapore	[θ], [ð], [r]	Articulation exercises, particularly fricative consonants; give enough time to every syllable; connect sounds together
Czech and Slovak	Czech Republic, Slovakia	[w], [kw], [r], [θ+ð], [æ], [I]	Do not lengthen vowels in second unstressed syllables. Avoid using [a:] for [æ]

Main world language	Key countries where it is spoken	Particularly difficult English sounds	Recommendations
Dutch	Holland, S. Africa	[r], [s], [θ], [ð], [əʊ]	
Farsi	Iran Afghanistan Pakistan	[θ], [ð], [w], [v], [æ]	Avoid adding [e] before [s]
French	France, Canada	[r], [iː], [j], []	Avoid nasalisation of vowels when followed by [n] or [ŋ]. Anglicise words of French origin
German	Austria Germany Switzerland	[w], [r], [æ], [əʊ], [v], [s], [z]	Be careful with voiced vs. unvoiced consonants
Greek	Greece	[dʒ], [tʃ]	
Hungarian	Hungary	[r], [w], [θ], [ð], [əʊ]	
Italian	Italy	[r], [θ], [ð], [t], [d], lateral plosion	Care needed on unstressed syllables and unpronounced letters
Japanese	Japan	[l], [r], [θ], [ð], [ʒ], [t], [d], [əʊ], [ɜː], [s], [z]	Give enough time for each syllable

Main world language	Key countries where it is spoken	Particularly difficult English sounds	Recommendations
Korean	Korea	[v], [f], [p], [b], [l], [r], [θ], [ð], [z]	Articulation exercises
Malay	Indonesia Malaysia	[əʊ], [ɔ:], [ɜ:], [æ], [θ], [ð], [ʃ], [ʒ]	Avoid over-pronouncing syllable clusters
Mongolian	Mongolia	[j], [l], [dʒ], [ʒ]	
Nigerian	Nigeria	[r], [θ+ð], [ə], [ʌ], [ɜ:], [v]	Avoid nasalization of vowels before final [n] + [m]
Norwegian	Norway	[dʒ], [kw], [θ], [ð]	Work on voiced consonants
Polish	Poland	[l], [r], [w], [θ], [ð]	
Portuguese	Portugal, Brazil	[dʒ], [ʒ], [tʃ], [θ], [ð], [w], [æ]	Articulate endings, particularly endings spelt as 'y'; avoid nasalization of vowels when followed by [m], [n]

Main world language	Key countries where it is spoken	Particularly difficult English sounds	Recommendations
Russian	Russia, CIS countries	[w], [l], [əʊ], [æ]	Avoid shortening long vowels, diphthongs, over-pronouncing consonants
Serbo-Croatian	Balkan countries	[r], [l], [æ], [e], [θ+ð], [w]	Avoid de-voicing final voiced consonants
South Asian Languages	India Pakistan Bangladesh Nepal	[r], [w], [æ], [əʊ]	Need to weaken the [r] sound
Spanish	Spain Latin America	[b], [v], [w], [h], [j], [r], [z]	Be sure to give full value to endings of words, and pronounce final consonants
Swahili	Tanzania Kenya Uganda Zaire	Long and short vowels	
Swedish	Sweden	[w], [dʒ], [s], [z]	Work on voiced consonants
Turkish	Turkey	[θ], [ð], [r]	Avoid over-pronouncing consonants

Bibliography

Anthropology of British Tongue-Twisters by K. Parkin, Samuel French Ltd, 1969

The Complete Annotated Gilbert and Sullivan, Oxford University Press, 1996

Learner English by M. Swan and B. Smith, Cambridge University Press, 2001

Old Oxford Book of Verses and Tongue-twisters, Oxford University Press, 1969

Practical Phonetics by J.C.Wells and Greta Colson, Pitman, 1971

English Pronouncing Dictionary by Daniel Jones, Cambridge University Press, 1977

Clear Speech by Malcolm Morrison A. and C. Black. 1977

Modern English Pronunciation Practice by M.D. Munro Mackenzie, Longman, 1967

The Voice Book by Michael McCallion, Faber and Faber, 1988

English Phonetics and Phonology by Peter Roach, Cambridge University Press, 1983

The Right to Speak by Patsy Rodenburg, Methuen, 1992

CD Contents

The symbol **A1** 🎧 indicates the CD and track number of recorded material – such as CD A, track 1. In the table, the track number on the CD is followed by the exercise number from the book.

CD A

1	A1	34	A34	67	A67
2	A2	35	A35	68	A68
3	A3	36	A36	69	A69
4	A4	37	A37	70	A70
5	A5	38	A38	71	A71
6	A6	39	A39	72	A72
7	A7	40	A40	73	A73
8	A8	41	A41	74	A74
9	A9	42	A42	75	A75
10	A10	43	A43	76	A76
11	A11	44	A44	77	A77
12	A12	45	A45	78	B1
13	A13	46	A46	79	B2
14	A14	47	A47	80	B3
15	A15	48	A48	81	B4
16	A16	49	A49	82	B5
17	A17	50	A50	83	B6
18	A18	51	A51	84	B7
19	A19	52	A52	85	B8
20	A20	53	A53	86	B9
21	A21	54	A54	87	B10
22	A22	55	A55	88	B11
23	A23	56	A56	89	B12
24	A24	57	A57	90	B13
25	A25	58	A58	91	B14
26	A26	59	A59	92	B15
27	A27	60	A60	93	B16
28	A28	61	A61	94	B17
29	A29	62	A62	95	B18
30	A30	63	A63	96	B19
31	A31	64	A64	97	B20
32	A32	65	A65		
33	A33	66	A66		

CD B

1	B21	33	B53	65	B85
2	B22	34	B54	66	B86
3	B23	35	B55	67	B87
4	B24	36	B56	68	B88
5	B25	37	B57	69	B89
6	B26	38	B58	70	B90
7	B27	39	B59	71	B91
8	B28	40	B60	72	B92
9	B29	41	B61	73	B93
10	B30	42	B62	74	B94
11	B31	43	B63	75	B95
12	B32	44	B64	76	B96
13	B33	45	B65	77	B97
14	B34	46	B66	78	B98
15	B35	47	B67	79	B99
16	B36	48	B68	80	B100
17	B37	49	B69	81	B101
18	B38	50	B70	82	B102
19	B39	51	B71	83	B103
20	B40	52	B72	84	B104
21	B41	53	B73	85	C1
22	B42	54	B74	86	C2
23	B43	55	B75	87	C3
24	B44	56	B76	88	C4
25	B45	57	B77	89	C5
26	B46	58	B78	90	C6
27	B47	59	B79	91	C7
28	B48	60	B80	92	C8
29	B49	61	B81		
30	B50	62	B82		
31	B51	63	B83		
32	B52	64	B84		

Glossary

General

Articulation – The exercising and thus strengthening of the speech organs to produce sharp, crisp consonants, leading to good clear diction.

Intonation – The rise and fall of the voice in speaking.

International Phonetic Alphabet – An alphabet of symbols representing sounds.

Phonetics – The science concerned with the study of speech processes, including the production, reception and analysis of speech sounds.

Voice Modulation - Variation in the strength, tone or pitch of one's voice.

Sounds

Vowels – A vowel is a voiced sound which has a free passage of breath through the mouth and is shaped by different positions of the lips and tongue. There are twelve pure English vowels – five long and seven short.

Diphthongs – A diphthong is a voiced sound consisting of two vowel sounds glided together. There are eight diphthongs in English.

Triphthongs – A triphthong is a voiced sound consisting of three vowel sounds glided together. There are three triphthongs in English.

Semi-vowels – Speech organs start in the position of one vowel and immediately move to another vowel. e.g. [w], [j].

Consonants – A consonant is a sound formed by partially or completely stopping the breath stream anywhere between the larynx and the lips. There are several categories of consonants:

1. **Plosives** – The passage is completely blocked by speech organs, pressure is built up, and on sudden release an explosive sound or "plosion" is heard. e.g. [p]-[b], [t]-[d], [k]-[g].

2. **Glottal Stop** – A sound made when the vocal chords are closed tightly, not allowing air to flow through (like holding your breath or lifting something heavy).

3. **Nasal** – A sound formed by complete closure of the mouth, the soft palate being lowered, so that air is free to pass out through the nose. e.g. [m], [n], [ŋ].

4. **Lateral** - Air escapes round the sides of a blockage (tip of the tongue on the alveolar ridge). e.g. [l].

5. **Fricatives** - The air passage is narrowed so that the air in escaping produces audible friction or a kind of hissing sound. e.g. [f]-[v], [s]-[z], [h], [r], [θ] - [ð], [ʃ]-[ʒ].

6. **Affricates** – Have the first part Plosive followed immediately by the second part Fricative. e.g. [tʃ] - [dʒ].

Acknowledgements

Among the many people to whom we are grateful for help in the preparation of this book, we must single out Marianne Gibson, Michael Knowles and Francesca Lett. We must say a special thank you to our chief editor Bud Smith for providing endless help and support throughout this project.

We also would like to thank the following reviewers from different cultural backgrounds who helped with feedback and piloting during the development of this project:

- Tim Matthew and Benjamin Beaumont, Oxford House College, London
- Diana Arama, Russia
- Beate M. Rissbacher, Austria
- Josephine Finn, Kogan Page publishers, London
- We also thank many foreign students from Mongolia, Poland, Iran, Germany, France, Italy, Turkey and Greece who helped during our marketing research in preparation of this book.

Cover design by Ben Strawbridge

Diagrams design by George Barco

Illustrations from *Big Book of Old-Time Spot Illustrations*, edited by Hayward Cirker.